Facing the Blank Page

A Collection of Essays and Poems
from the First Ten Years of *Fine Lines*,
a Literary Journal, 1992-2001

David Martin

Published by WriteLife, LLC
7914 W. Dodge Rd.
Suite 384
Omaha, NE 68114
www.writelife.com

Printed in the United States of America

Photo Credits:
front cover photograph, Bent Georg Nordeng
back cover photograph, Andrey Mikityuk

ISBN 978 1 60808 005 2

First Edition

Acclaim for David Martin's

Facing the Blank Page

A Collection of Essays and Poems

from the First Ten Years of *Fine Lines*,

a Literary Journal, 1992-2001

"These essays are an interesting journey from introspective curiosity about what makes Martin's soul tick to excellent narratives about motivating one to write. The consistent goal of these reflections is what makes people string sentences together and how we can encourage ourselves and others to make writing a habit. As a result of his constant urging, good writers evolve and constantly make the *Fine Lines* publication an exciting quarterly journal full of poetry, humor, short stories, and personal revelation."

-Richard Koelling, retired government employee

"A teacher, a writer, and a man who believes in the strength of a networking writing community, Martin's *Fine Lines* quarterly journal includes writers of all ages who share prose and poetry. It is nice to know that such a place exists where my high school students and their teacher can write, revise, and submit our work for consideration. Martin's essays cover a wide range of topics, but I am drawn to them, because of his keen eye for observation and the exquisite shaping of words and language. I read his writing to my classes as examples of an inspiring tone, style, and purpose. I am excited to see a book of his fine-tuned essays, a showcase from a man who believes in the power of written art."

-Deborah McGinn, Lincoln High School, Lincoln, NE

"Martin has the rare gift of writing in such a way as to inspire the readers to open their eyes and look more closely at the world around them. Whatever subject he writes about, he convinces us that he has discovered what is most important in life and has never forgotten it. He epitomizes Plato's famous quotation from Socrates: 'The unexamined life is not worth the living.' At the heart of his essays is Martin's conviction that writing is essential to the well being of people of all ages, and his journal *Fine Lines* transcends generational boundaries. Martin has found joy and meaning in his own writing, and he is passionate in his desire to encourage others to realize what a precious gift writing can be. In *Walden,* Henry David Thoreau wrote 'What a miracle it would be if we could see through another's eyes if only for an instant.' Martin's essays are a fulfillment of that miracle, and the view is clear and life-affirming. His essays model what I believe the concept of 'fine lines' means: a graceful style, a strong voice, a facility with language, and a focus on what is significant in life."

-Dr. Loren Logsdon, Professor of English, Eureka College, IL

"In the Emersonian tradition, Martin's essays explore the human spirit. Like a quintessential modern essayist, he uses the raw material of his own life to express what is universal in each of us. I am delighted to see the essays I have read through the years in one book where I can turn the pages, taste the ideas, and savor!"

-Colleen Aagesen, co-author of *Shakespeare for Kids*

"Spawned by the need to engage disenfranchised students, *Fine Lines* has grown far beyond the expectations of the inner city, high school teacher who first asked his students to write about their lives. Martin could not have foreseen the impact this classroom assignment would have on his students, and no one could have predicted the success of the literary magazine that began as a compilation of their stories. From the earliest student essays to the most recent edition of *Fine Lines*, the one constant has been Martin's relentless devotion and candid, heartfelt words. This collection of his contributions over the years is a tribute to the man, as well as the journal he created."

-James A. Hale, Jr., Union Pacific Corporation

"Martin is more than just a talented writer with the ability to blend the profound essence of philosophy with the right touch of spirituality. He is also the Grand Marshal of a parade of aspiring poets and writers marching toward the capture of those elusive answers to the questions of 'Who are we?' and 'What is our purpose here?' "

-Darrel Draper, Historical Speaker and Entertainer

"These essays open up one's mind to all sorts of possibilities. Martin's writing takes the reader on various journeys. Through his thoughtful perspectives, commentaries, and creative musings, I find myself contemplating my own writing more. After reading his writing, I am inclined to cruise into areas that I once felt insecure with as a writer. Through good imagery and thoughtful content, it is wonderful to absorb the author's purpose, and simultaneously derive pure literary enjoyment. I achieve both from these essays. Martin is devoted to his calling and is an inspiration to fledgling writers and diehards in the field."

-Mary Bannister, Language Arts Teacher, Albion, NY

"I look forward to the publication of Martin's collected works. These personal stories speak to the struggle of one who was called to write and was redeemed by his own words. His works reflect a profound love of the writing process. Eighteen years as the creator and publisher of *Fine Lines* is his testimony to the world. He believes that everyone has a story to tell. Writing is a creative and healing act. He listens with empathy and acceptance; then, out of respect for and in honor of the challenges in life, he declares, 'Write on!' "

-Dr. Janet Waage Lingren, EdD, LMHP, CPC

"I was able to fulfill my passion for writing poetry because Martin encouraged and praised me. More than anything, I was inspired by his passion for writing. He is thoughtful, reflective, compassionate, and motivates students to do their best in pursuit of truth and accuracy. Hundreds of young writers are blessed in the *Fine Lines* summer camps he organizes, because he has a way of compelling them to share their lives on paper. He has taught writing courses, elementary school through college for thirty years, and thousands of writers have emerged from this city and state because of him."

-Wendy Lundeen, Buffett Magnet School, Omaha, NE

"Martin's depth and thoughtfulness as a teacher and a writer have inspired thousands throughout his career. His passion for writing and his ability to take the least interested writers and make them believe in themselves enough to submit their own work for publication has been phenomenal to watch. *Fine Lines*, once only a dream of his, is now a well-respected publication across the country. I'm proud to say he's inspired me to write, as well!"

-Cara Riggs, Principal, Omaha South High School, Omaha, NE

"Eighteen years ago, Martin told me he was experimenting in his English composition classes with the idea to have his students' written work 'published,' so they could see their work in print. His students were thrilled, wanting to write more in hopes it would appear in his newsletter. He started *Fine Lines* to encourage writers of all ages. The publication expanded to national and international distribution. It published elementary students to senior citizens. What I noticed over those years is that the pieces written by Martin himself were splendid, always well-written, provocative, original, and in a style so unique one wanted to read what he had to say. His work needs to be shared with others. His insights, thoughts, compassion, and ability to speak to all are gifts that readers will, no doubt, find relevant to their lives."

-Dr. Bruce Baker, Professor of English, UNO, Omaha, NE

"*Fine Lines* IS a classroom, and its editor is the teacher. Students naturally learn language in a vertical proficiency group, not just from reading the best that has been thought and written, but from the writers who are a little ahead of them in proficiency as well as from those who are well ahead of them. Even more important is the insight that language learners and novice writers need models, not correctors, and Martin as the editor/teacher provides that model in the essays he has provided in *Fine Lines*. How many writing classes are contexts in which the learners never see a more mature writer writing? Paradoxically, Martin corrects that by modeling, not by correcting! There is so much to be learned about learning to write by studying carefully what he has done as editor/teacher in writing essays for his own publication, *Fine Lines*."

-Dr. Les Whipp, Professor of English, Emeritus, UNL, Lincoln, NE

"In his collection of personal essays, Martin gives us no less than a series of prescriptions for how to conduct an examined life. Most of his exhortations involve writing and learning, and he often links these two processes tightly. 'I Think; Therefore, I Write,' he says. *Learn Blissfully* is another essay advising us to follow our passions joyfully, while overcoming obstacles like a challenging teacher or difficult material. Writing itself is Martin's most important subject and process. 'I help shape my destiny by learning to shape the sentences I use. Life speaks for itself, but I listen with my journal.' A writer's writer, Martin assures others in *Facing the Blank Page* that a clean page becomes a new adventure and a humble prayer of understanding. Frequently, Martin uses objects like a garden or his room or a window as metaphors for the writer's life. Readers will find Martin's essays charming and inspiring; they will find him a generous teacher and a beguiling companion; a model and an inspiration. With his encouragement and example, would-be writers will discover, 'Yes, we can!' "

-Dr. J.J. McKenna, Professor of English, UNO, Omaha, NE

"Martin is a storyteller whose passion for the written word produces masterfully crafted prose. His search for universal truths elevates and enlightens the reader. This collection of his work, like fine chocolate, should be savored."

-Sharon R. Spartz, Minnesota writer

"A life-long teacher, Martin leads his students and readers through the soul-searching required for good writing. In these essays, he shares his personal journey and some of his techniques for encouraging even the most reluctant writer. With a gift for focusing on the positive, the good, and the inspirational, he guides us in the fruitful pursuit of our own journeys and our own writing."

-Laura Neece-Baltaro, Nebraska poet

"Writing from the heart with an experienced perspective, Martin uses words to paint the hues and textures of his life's journey."

-Dr. Della Meyer, Adjunct Professor, Peru State College, Peru, NE

"I have been inspired by Martin's essays. He encourages: 'Continue to dream tolerance into this world. Give hope.' He is a writer's writer and writer's editor. His voice is one of diversity, texture, and optimism. For Martin, it is all about words. 'Write On!' "

-David Prinz Hufford, IWCC, Council Bluffs, IA

"Martin started *Fine Lines* with a Jeffersonian motivation to extend free expression to young students marginalized by school and society, which also gave inspiration to those who worked creatively in the teaching of writing. The journal is now an outlet not only for students and their writing teachers, who are given the pride of publication, but also for persons of all ages and professions with a penchant for open expression. *Fine Lines* grew out of his perception, not always understood even among teachers, that writing is a communal process where all who use a language have equal access to its resources and an equal chance of hitting on an insight which enriches everyone's sense of human possibility. I have enjoyed the student work in *Fine Lines* for its unself-conscious joy in finding a way to say something personally important and worth sharing. Not every reader recognizes the extent to which Martin's writing inspires the contributors and determines the direction of the writing in *Fine Lines*. His writings sound so direct and honest that they seem spontaneous, but anyone who writes regularly will recognize the art which produced them. It is one thing to recognize the person behind the writing as generous and empathetic; it is another to be moved in an open environment, to reach the readers and writers of the community."

-Dr. Robert Haller, Founding President, Academic Freedom Coalition of Nebraska

I dedicate this book to

my wife, Yolie,

and children: Bradley, Ashley, and Erin.

Without their warm support, encouragement, constant questions, proof-reading skills, expanding vision, and sincerity, this work would not have been completed. As I listen to them, I hear the music in my life that is the most inspirational to me. They are great souls who value words in their own ways and allow me to create myself, line by line, page by page.

Acknowledgments

"Life isn't about finding yourself.
Life is about creating yourself."

-E. W. Wilcox

I have a debt of gratitude that I owe to many people. The list of those who supported me in accomplishing this task is long. Because they let me stand on their broad shoulders, I was able to see over the horizon and create myself with these words.

Dr. Les Whipp, English professor at the University of Nebraska-Lincoln, taught me what the Nebraska Writing Project was about in 1979, showed me different ways to teach non-traditional writing students just like myself, and introduced me to my future wife in one of his classes.

Dr. Bruce Baker, English professor at the University of Nebraska-Omaha, became my graduate school adviser, and then he decided to remain in that capacity for the rest of his life.

Dr. John McKenna, Co-Director, Graduate Certificate in Advanced Writing, at the University of Nebraska-Omaha, provided an unlimited supply of good teaching examples. On a daily basis, he demonstrated the beauty and strength of a well-written declarative sentence.

Thanks to the Nebraska Writing Project for allowing me to enter their network of writers. With their inspiration and creativity, I renewed myself, continuously.

Harold Mann is a relentless man. He would not let me rest until this collection was finished.

For almost two decades, my friends at *Fine Lines* let me use their energy and volunteerism to build our own writing network that publishes "new writers of all ages." These hard workers help produce each issue of our non-profit publication: Steve Gehring, Tom Pappas, David Mainelli, Rich Knapp, Kim Bultsma, Laura Neece Baltaro, Wendy Lundeen, Jayne Schlosser, Marty Pierson, Bernice Nared, Rose Gleisberg, Joyce Dunn, Deb Derrick, Bev Crouter, Betty Segell, Jan Sutherland, Jay Worden, Kay Bret,

Raleigh Wilkerson, Patricia Schicker, Joyce Dunn, Anne James, Richard Koelling, Stan Maliszewski, Mary Bannister, Jessica Bieler, Sheila Boerner, Brigid Freymuller, Edie Goodwin, Loren Logsdon, Deborah McGinn, Judy Lorenzen, Dorothy Miller, Elizabeth Pesek, Jack Pettit, John Robinson, Julie Temple, Marion Young, and Anna Schmidt.

Cindy Grady, Managing Director, and the WriteLife, LLC Team (WriteLife.com), provided the publication direction I needed to transform these words into a book. I support their philosophy that everybody has at least one book to write, and WriteLife, LLC, wants to bring those books to light.

The many students who filled my classes, year after year, taught me the most important lesson a teacher can learn. Every person has a story to tell. Listen. Listen. Listen.

To you all, I am most grateful.

David Martin
Omaha, Nebraska

Contents

Introduction

Ideas are like "butterflies," and my journal is a net. I open its pages to capture them one at a time. Then, I string words together, using those ideas until the joy becomes contagious. The required discipline is to "just begin."

If I remember to appreciate and play with these "butterflies," I no longer fear facing the blank page in front of me. The good ones and the ugly ones are all important. There are no bad ideas, because each is capable of transforming a reader in some degree. The truth will appear, when I write enough. The mission is to "just write."

Finding the will to place my "butterflies" on paper has changed my life in many ways. It allowed me the freedom to be myself, gave me the endurance to overcome challenges, and encouraged me to see the world through different lenses. With these metaphorical glasses, I stopped concentrating on the past and turned to look at the sunrise.

Tomorrow

I was stuck in the past,
trapped in square memories,
pressured by suits and smiles,
and always colored inside the lines.

What I really wanted
was to heal old wounds,
dream the real me,
and last until tomorrow.

Writing of life's experiences brings order to chaos, beauty to existence, and celebration to the mysterious. Hopefully, words connected to actions will make a difference. How can they not? Don't we all need a more positive world to share? Let's begin our dream of that possibility right now.

This collection of essays and poems is my humble attempt to write my way home. They began as memories from experiences long past, then became current emotions that continue to shake up my orchard of bliss, and a few are recognizable dreams to which I awake each morning, delirious with the expectation that they have come true, at last.

1

A Writer's Prayer

Great Spirit!
You give me a reason for being,
a sense of mission in this life.
I see small accomplishments and realize
there is purpose behind them.

My creativity is a gift from You.
I recognize these blessings,
increasingly, more and more each day.
I know I am on the right path.

Guide me, and give me strength
to reach my distant goals.
I search for peace in my writing
and trust others will find happiness there.

You will guide those who listen.
I look to my writing in hopes of seeing visions,
those windows You open for me.
I ask for wisdom.

Touch my shoulder and guide me.
I pray to hear Your voice in the silence of the night,
in the noise of confusion,
and with the terror of the blank page.

2

Dragon Slayers

"Good writing is
clear thinking made visible."

–Bill Wheeler

It is now 3 a.m. Noise pounds in my head. Flashes of thoughts light the darkness of my world. I am tired and cannot sleep.

An awful dragon chased me for 5 ½ hours tonight. Our battle sounded like the thunder and looked like the lightning of my dreams. I heard my sword crash against the fire breathing monster's neck, and I awoke to hear real monsters clash with Zeus' bolts of fire in the sky.

Outside, Mother Nature's rain falls softly. Nature's real thunder and lightning keep calling my attention to life's rebirth, baptismal cleansing, and regeneration. It's never too late to start over.

The monster of my dreams aroused the emotional "thunder" and "lightning" that took place, yesterday, at our monthly Dragon Slayer's meeting. Those flashes of sound and insights of truth now stir me to write once again.

Our meeting's discussion went from patience to parking lots, nuclear holocaust to Nikki Giovanni, a search for passion to paternalism, Native American desires to Nietzsche, individual courage to Camus, an early morning swim to Schopenhauer, and a quest for real education to erudition. My mind became excited and tired, as a result of our four hours of sharing. There is much electricity in this group of writers. It is no wonder that "Donder" and "Blitzen" now mean more to me than just two names of Santa's reindeer.

If Giovanni said there are no conversations, just intersecting monologues, what would she say about Sunday afternoon? Our sharing and discussion proved good exposition and feedback occur when writers commit to their tasks.

No one really knows the mind and soul of another. Friend, husband, wife, child - do we really know who the other person is? Probably not, but yesterday's attempt was a huge beginning. Let the flow of written words never stop, as we follow our quest to write ourselves into our destiny.

"I can feel again . . . there but for the grace . . . it is the moments I like . . . memories last longer than the experiences . . . suffer in order to create . . . passion rules . . . courage and content . . . dare to go over the edge . . . look at the eye of the tiger . . . don't blink . . . it is a question of vision . . . a search for the truth . . . dare to rebel . . . personal battlegrounds call for priorities . . . life is a struggle to be authentic . . . ."

These glimpses of everyone's participation are sparks for much contemplation and great writing. Don't be satisfied to talk about them. Write them down. Develop them before they vanish. We must challenge our dragons before they disappear.

I use to spend so much time worrying about the "boo-boos" I made, the people I hurt, and the opportunities I lost that I only made myself depressed. When I learned that my depression was only sublimated, personal anger, I decided I was not progressing by hurting myself, so I stopped it. I am only human. Yes, I made mistakes. I will make more, I am sure, but I don't want to dwell on them. I choose to think of the future, to emphasize that aspect of my life, to accentuate the positive things I can influence. These things, I know, will be affected by my attention.

I try not to worry about the past. What is done is done. Just let me learn from the past and move on. I pray I don't repeat the same errors, and I hope to move to a higher ground. Then, if I make more mistakes, at least, they will be new ones.

Living is endless "being," a continuous growth. There is no finish line, just life in a marathon and small victories tacked onto each other. Each ending is a new beginning. I try to keep my eyes on the road and relax behind the wheel. Instead of going around and around in circles repeating the same mistakes of the past, if I can slowly, continuously, move to a higher level, my circles will become spirals. That is good enough for me.

The only responsibility a river has is to flow to the sea. I don't have to be anything else but the river I was created to be. My mission is to simply live what I am. If I am the Missouri, I don't have to be the Amazon. If I don't do what the Missouri is supposed to do, that is my only mistake.

Rivers don't go upstream. I don't have to push the current. The river will flow by itself. Its job is simply to be patient, take the curves and bends as they come, and ride, ride, ride to the sea.

The Greeks said happiness was attaining perfect balance and moderation in all things. When I am not happy, I find that parts of my life are more emphasized than others. Often, I notice my unhappiness comes about when I am thinking only of myself. When I want something so badly, I think of nothing else. When I am obsessed by possessing a material item, when I am greedy, my displeasure with life is at its peak.

When I quit worrying about the getting, when I begin thinking about the giving, my happiness returns. When I am aware of serving others or something larger than myself, when I volunteer my time, when I let good things pass through me to someone else, my happiness returns. It is not the taking that is important; it's the touching. It is not the getting that counts; it is the giving.

If someone asked me, "What are the Dragon Slayers all about?" I would say they are about all of the above and more. Individuals have their own personal dragons to overcome. According to Joseph Campbell, we may have more than one. The dragons can be many things: possessions, fears, ideas, jobs, school, teachers, wives, husbands, children, and egos. The monsters are concerns in life that prevent us from being ourselves and pursuing those things that let us become happy.

Campbell used the idea of following one's bliss to find true happiness and defeat one's dragons. In our lives, metaphorical dragons block our paths and prevent us from going down our very own yellow-brick road to Oz, where we will surely be able to find ourselves a brain, a heart, and the courage we need to be successful.

Dragon Slayers travel the road of life searching for its truth through writing. Once the truth, as we see it, is found, the next step requires action. Knowledge is the knowing, but wisdom is knowledge in motion. We want to do more than just find the dragons. Going past those monsters to a better emotional and physical world creates the thunder and lightning that I hear. Let's confront those dragons. Let's keep our faith! Let's write on!

3

Facing the Blank Page

"Books – the best antidote against
the marsh-gas of boredom and vacuity."

–George Steiner

Much of my time is spent teaching students how to write effectively, and I enjoy it. The more I teach writing the more joy I receive. Sometimes, I wonder why I like this challenge and so many others do not. Why is it that a blank sheet of paper compels me to fill it with words? Putting my thoughts on paper cleanses me mentally, like exercise cleanses me physically. Writing is not a competitive sport, but it is a demanding activity. Composition insists on the dedication of time and concentration, but writing is a forgiving endeavor. I eliminate mistakes by starting over with a clean sheet of paper.

Most people think writing is work, and when I listen to some students from past classes, it is the most difficult work possible. I admit that some of my own school and college classes were filled with mental anguish and physical boredom. Demons of masochism danced inside my head when I prepared a research paper assignment forced upon me. Only later, when I began writing for myself did it become enjoyable. Now, I hurry to a pen when I hear something that stirs me. John Cheever said, "The pleasure of writing is unequaled." A few years ago, I would not have shared this opinion, but now I most certainly do.

A simple person enjoys simple pleasures. Writing is one of those simple exercises that adds to my life. It allows time and opportunity to share my feelings and passion for living. Writing is one of the most intimate forms of communication. Because of this intimacy, I live my life with the maximum amount of pleasure. The older I get, the more I realize that life should not be measured by its length but by the depth one explores it. Writing increases the intensity of my life.

A clean page becomes a new adventure, a mirror of the mind's thoughts, and a humble prayer of understanding. In the same way that a prayer cannot be taught, the essence of writing cannot be taught. Placing a collection of symbols on paper is a symbol itself. The fundamentals may be learned but not the abstraction. In the way that praying is looking for God and Divine answers, writing is looking for self and introspective answers. Both are gifts not to be overlooked and ignored.

Many revered prophets went into the desert to meditate. They found their answers and desired atonement. Their respective deserts provided a removal of excess nonsense. It was a time to seek the truth. People always search for ways to begin fresh. We want to receive forgiveness and grace. We want a renewal of faith in ourselves. We want a clean start. Saints, heretics, and writers have a lot in common besides the suffering and sacrifice that go with their positions.

Similar to prophets finding truth in the desert, writers see ideas and feelings on blank pages. The sheet of paper acts like a catcher's mitt and traps the different pitches of the heart and mind. The writing triggers the bullets of ideas to shoot out of the writer's pen, like a gun, and strike the 8 1/2" by 11" targets in rows and paragraphs.

I heard some priests talking about the desert. One said, "If one lives there long enough, one risks meeting God." Writers risk similar discoveries. If they write long enough, they risk finding themselves. A prophet's desert is found anywhere. It does not have to be in a geographic location, and a writer's tools come from many sources.

To find his salvation, a priest must take a leap of faith and cross the barriers of ignorance and death. A writer takes a leap of faith to transcend the fears of mediocrity and writer's block. Religious people abandon themselves to their gods. Writers abandon themselves to their work. To stop writing is to stop growing and to stop the process of self-discovery.

Writing is similar to motherhood with its pain and suffering to bring a child into the world. The agony of creating anything, children or an essay, is an art. The human embryo is in the dark for nine months. How long have some of the world's writers been "in the dark," until their "babies" were delivered into the light? Anne Frank? Papillion? Solzhenitsyn? Growth comes in the dark for all living things, whether they are children or writers' manuscripts.

Writing is like farming. The seeds grow in the soul, and the germination period of despair forces the words upward toward the light of exposure. The sheet of paper becomes a plowed field, prepared and planted. The seeds sown in symmetrical rows soon bloom and become ideas. With a final draft or a published manuscript, the crop is harvested.

I am impressed by writers who know it is important to write rough drafts, then revise and rewrite when necessary. Young writers who are afraid to revise their first attempts should remember this saying: "Of course, God created man before he created woman. Any artist knows you have to make the rough draft before you can finish the original masterpiece" (Anonymous).

I am surprised by writers who have the foresight to achieve brevity of thought. I like writers who can say what they have to say succinctly. Lengthy writing does not ensure quality or permanency.

"Did you know that there are only fifty-six words in The Lord's Prayer, 266 words in Lincoln's Gettysburg Address, and 297 words in The Ten Commandments? However, in a recent US government release of a federal study on the price of cabbages, the document contained 26,911 words" (Harry Wong).

I hope to see students achieve a curiosity of inquiry about the writing process and how it allows them to discover themselves. The process eliminates the games people play in covering up their true natures.

Keeping a journal hones mechanical skills, sharpens wits, increases clarity of thinking, and reduces the chances of self-deception. What goes onto the page in front of the writer is part of the creator. We owe it to ourselves never to give up hope that what we write, or attempt to produce, will benefit someone, if not another then ourselves.

The following applies most importantly to writers and their process of self-discovery: "It is not so much that I value discourse to others that is right and clear and graceful . . . as that practice in such discourse is the only way of assuring that one says things rightly and courteously and powerfully to oneself" (Jerome Bruner).

Is there a better reason for writing? The best audience writers have is themselves. To work, to learn, and to write are privileges many people do not enjoy. The difference between good writing and making anything perfectly is only material. Good writing is an act of simplicity. It is stripped of surroundings and excess trappings, just the pen, the paper, and the writer. If writers do not like the way things turn out, their patience and tolerance will let them begin again. Welcome to the adventure. When a writer faces the blank page, life is filled with hope and opportunity.

4

In My Bliss

"The time to read is any time:
no appointment . . . is necessary."

-Holbrook Jackson

Some people read books to discover the souls of others. I write to discover my own. I want to discover who I am. Few things in life teach me who I am more than writing in my journal does. This desire for self-knowledge inspires me to write almost every day.

Seldom do I lack the inspiration to write, but I often lose my focus. I spend too much time doing many things other than writing. Earning money, pursuing life's pleasures, and trying to please others all cause me to get lost in the fog of daily existence. I get tired making a living in a stressful environment. I feel waves of people, emotions, and work wash over me and knock me off my feet. I search for my footing in my journal. I look for meaningful reflections in my sentences and metaphors, and my journal becomes a symbol, revealing my true self. I want to be good at a few things in life. Conveying accurate images through my choice of words is one of them. I want to use my gifts well.

Simple things in life inspire me to write. My heart lifts when I see a male cardinal in a bare, winter tree above mounds of white snow. My soul warms when I see a strong, male hand hold a tiny child's fragile fingers. Fathers teaching sons and daughters the sacrifices needed to reach maturity turn my pages. Lovers looking into each other's eyes inspire me to paint the scene with words. Close friends sitting together, silently drinking coffee, as they watch moisture form on a window, while the cold, Nebraska wind howls outside, these images warm me to the possibilities.

When friendly eyes locate me in a crowded room, I am urged to write. When loved ones bare their souls to me, I look for a pen. When a student comes to class with the attitude, "I am ready to learn today, and you can teach me," I open my notebook.

I write while eating gumbo, listening to Cajun music. I look for pen and paper when I hear "Silent Night" fill the air on Christmas Eve. I sit down under a tree to record my emotions when my daughter chooses, on her own, to take the training wheels off and ride her bicycle solo for the first time. When Ray Charles sings "Georgia," when Beethoven plays "Moonlight Sonata," and when the little, blue engine finally gets over the mountain, they all speak to me in the same way. I cannot pass up these opportunities to think in ink.

When my work captivates me, when I hear, "Daddy, I love you," when I see outstretched hands reaching for a baby's face, when I feel soft fingers on my shoulder, when I hear the words, "Everything will be all right, now. I am here with you," I am fortunate, if I can put half of what I feel onto paper.

When I remember my writing passions, I stay on the path meant for me. These times inspire me to write, and I am content in my bliss.

5

I Think; Therefore, I Write

"Build yourself a book-nest
to forget the world without."

–Abraham Cowley

A person with a good education is able to use the past to prepare visions of beauty for the future. When Picasso sat in front of a blank canvas, he did what all writers must do when they face the blank page. They must make something from nothing.

Writers must see the world with the eyes of a child, the newness, the freshness, the miraculous, to improve the way we see life and ourselves, to make a poem out of each day, carpe diem.

> "Youth is happy because it has the ability to see beauty. Anyone who keeps the ability to see beauty never grows old" (Franz Kafka).
> "Cogito, Ergo Sum" (René Descartes).
> "I feel; therefore, I exist" (Thomas Jefferson).
> "I rebel; therefore, I am" (Albert Camus).
> "I ought; therefore, I can" (Immanuel Kant).
> "I want; therefore, I am" (Leo Tolstoy).
> "Sometimes, I think, and sometimes, I am" (Paul Valery).
> "I doubt; therefore, I believe" (Marshall Fishwick).
> "It was woman who taught me to say I am; therefore, I think" (George Bernard Shaw).
> "I party; therefore, I am" (Greg Gruber).

With my apologies to Descartes and others, we probably identify our personal search for beauty in life more closely with one of the above thoughts, but we come together as fellow Dragon Slayers to affirm the validity of the interpretation of these attempts to find the meaning of our earthly existence. We, as a group, acknowledge in one another our own struggles with questions about what it means to be alive.

A profound teacher of mine liked to say we all seek one person in life who we trust and one who will say, "I see you as you are. I hear you clearly, and I want to help you." When we find that mentor, confidant, or lover, only then will we learn who we really are. Only when writers change their life perspectives from "I" to "We" will they put into action what it means to be who we really are.

Sometimes, one must travel far to discover what is near. This lesson is taught in the wonderful children's book *The Treasure* by Uri Schulevitz. In this old folktale, the main character, Isaac, has three dreams (prayers) where he goes from his little village to the capital city to see the king in search of his personal fortune. Finally, he begins his journey on foot because he is so poor. When he gets to the palace, the king is on vacation and won't return for many days.

The Captain of the King's Guards watches Isaac deal with his frustration and despair. When the old man proves he is not a troublemaker, the Captain mentions something very surprising. The Captain tells of a dream he had the previous night about an old man who had an unknown treasure under the floor behind his stove at home. Isaac goes home to find the treasure that he sought in the palace behind the stove in his own home.

This story illustrates a basic truth few of us realize about our lives. The beauty in life, our treasure, is not in great places, in great adventures, or in great things. Our wealth is found in our ordinary lives, where we live each day. How we spend that treasure is the next question.

Education is putting reason to work. Using our intellect to make the choices we are called upon to make is the "stuff" of life. We must make these choices flower. To not make them produce is to ignore our creativity, and we must go with our best intentions and not look back.

"All the problems of the world could be settled easily if (people) were only willing to think. The trouble is that (people) very often resort to all sorts of devices in order not to think, because thinking is such hard work" (Nicholas Murray Butler, American educator, 1862-1947).

"There are few earthly things more beautiful than a university. It is a place where those who have ignorance may strive to know, where those who perceive truth may strive to make others see; where seekers and learners alike banded together in the search for knowledge, will honor thought in all its finer ways, will welcome thinkers in distress or in exile, will uphold the dignity of thought and learning and will exact standards in these things" (excerpt from a speech delivered by John Masefield at the University of Sheffield, England, 6/25/1946).

A well-functioning university or any good school is beautiful because a true education emancipates the students. Barriers collapse around the educated. Writing and the crafting of words liberate the heart and soul of the knowing. Education answers the question: Why should I care? Why should I be concerned? Enlightened people feel compassion, suffering, and engagement for those areas they understand.

Mankind craved drink long before it wanted to read books. How fitting that Gutenberg's first printing press was a converted wine press. Our basic, more primitive needs must be satisfied first, but the miraculous in education is to take the common, the primitive, and rise to a higher ground. Our use of words will accomplish this, rising up as much as a Steinbeck novel from pressed grapes.

Educated people must say what they mean and do what they say. Words are important and can demolish existential barriers. Uneducated people are trapped by mores, prisoners of their era and culture, and hobbled by societal norms. Educated people live simply and pride themselves on their self-reliance.

Why do people want an education in the first place: money, fame, security, prestige, power, or because they want to understand? A rich man whose pockets are lined with gold is not my primary example to follow in life. The person who dies with the most toys does not win the race I am running. Money is just another wall. Nothing changes for the rich. They live by themselves, believing their lives are better simply because their bank accounts are fatter.

In the world of nutrition, we now know that fat is the number one cause of physical illness in this country. Writers and artists who do not struggle to find the source of truth in their craft, those who sacrifice their art for an easy way out (more money, a softer position), those who yearn to be comfortable before creating, will live a shorter artistic life, just as the person who wallows in doughnuts and fried foods will live a shorter natural life. A prison by any other name is still a prison.

6

Keep the Faith

"When once the itch of literature has come over a man,
nothing will cure it but the scratching of a pen."

-Sam Lower

The more I write in my journal, the more I learn about the world and myself. The more I share my writing with my classes, the more open I become to my students, the more open they become to me, and the better all of our writing develops.

Often, I hear students refer to their feelings of isolation from family, friends, and other students. I sense they are stranded on a metaphorical desert island waiting for a passing steamer to rescue them. Sitting alone under a palm tree, sunburned, and tired of eating coconuts, their lives are blocked. Writing in a journal - one that takes on a personality of its own, one that becomes an extension of the author, one that holds the truth like notes placed in a bottle thrown into the Gulf Stream as a means of salvation - will help create that puff of smoke on the distant horizon indicating help is on the way.

Many times, students need to see themselves as unique individuals. Being different is the price we pay for being better. Following the herd creates a boring sameness, a death-like monotony, and keeps us from achieving our potential. Writing in a journal reflects back to us how truly original we are.

John Hancock Field said, "All worthwhile people have good thoughts, good ideas, and good inventions, but precious few of them ever translate those into actions."

I wait no more. Writing in a journal encourages me to translate my ideas into actions. If I can write about my ideas, I can see them as real possibilities. If I can capture them in a journal, I can refer to them later when I need to act on them.

Many students dwell on their negative life experiences, and most of us go through periods like this. When I have no one to listen to me, my journal becomes my best friend, my voice in the night, the big brother or sister I never had, and my guiding light. Often, simply writing my feelings onto a blank page helps me through the darkness.

The seventh century Chinese philosopher, Hui-neng, said, "The meaning of life is to see." Looking at something is not the same as seeing it. In our complicated world, we have so much to look at, but we see so little. Simply looking at things demeans life. Seeing things clearly gives life meaning.

Writing in a journal forces me to see things, not just look at them. I can't count how many students have told me that by simply writing devotedly in their journals they found meaning in their lives they didn't know existed.

One of the wisest men I know told me that everyone searches for the meaning of life. He said the answer is not to be found but created. If there is no particular purpose, we must develop one. Following our own unique destiny is challenging for all and frightening for many. When following our individual paths, we can't hide in the herd any longer. Keep the faith. Create yourself. Write on.

7

Learn Blissfully

"If a book comes from the heart,
it will contrive to reach other hearts."

-Thomas Carlyle

People spend too much time running away from things they should face. We run away from threatening people, embarrassing predicaments, scolding mothers, belligerent fathers, crying sisters, awkward brothers, boring husbands, silent wives, suffocating jobs, stifling homes, uninteresting schools, and tough homework. However, more people run away from themselves than from anyone or anything else.

Ralph Waldo Emerson said, "No thing is at last sacred, but the integrity of our own minds." If this is the case, most of us have little that is sacred, even less integrity, and we don't know our own minds. Fear of the unknown coupled with Franklin Delano Roosevelt made a great pair. Remember? "There is nothing we have to fear but fear itself." Emerson would have agreed with FDR. They both suggest that if we know our own minds, there will be nothing to fear after all.

I give myself notice. I accept the challenge. I will say the truth and live accordingly. This process will sting at times, but I vividly remember what it was like to live behind facades. I was afraid of trying new ideas; I did not enjoy each day. I wasted good friends, and I forgot how to live. I want the real me to be on the surface of life, swimming in the sunshine. I hope to be more like the "Sage of Concord" with my feet on the ground and my head in the air. I must make life's journey by myself. I may care for other people, but in the final analysis, I only learn what I teach myself.

I do not have to run anymore. I am not competing against anyone in this life. I am trying to achieve the true potential that resides in me. I go at my own pace. I don't have to be Gandhi or Jesus Christ. I only have to be myself.

I know I am a seeker. My drummer beats at a progressively different tune than many hear. I find it hard to pay attention to the rhythm that is in my mind alone, and it is hard to leave the herd and dance my own dance.

I was an average student in school. Infrequently, I would reach for an "A" and achieve it, when I felt motivated by the subject matter. I remember one day in twelfth grade, however, when I wanted to learn for the fun of learning. I wanted to absorb all I could about why the mind works the way it does. I also hoped to see the shocked surprise on the faces of those gifted girls who traveled with me all the way from kindergarten to high school graduation. Just once, I wanted to show them that I could beat them at their own game. I felt they thought they were much better than I was, and usually, they were. Most often, I didn't think I could compete with them, so I did not try, but this day was different.

Mrs. Kaiser's twelfth grade psychology class intrigued me. She was a big woman with a strong, German accent. A quiet and stern lady, she ruled her class with a no-nonsense approach to teaching. When she tried to smile, her lips formed a thin, straight line that barely curved at the corners. She never repeated herself twice, nor did she have to. Everyone listened intently rather than get burned by her piercing stare when a mistake was made. Everyday, the class valedictorian and salutatorian answered all her questions, while the rest of us watched.

One day, this tough teacher and human psychology both appeared warm and inviting. Something clicked inside me during the class discussion, and I started answering the questions she did not think to cover or the class all-stars did not mention. She looked at me in an odd way. She leaned her head to the side, and her reading glasses rose slightly, when she stopped talking to the class to look at me directly, coolly, without speaking.

I did nothing wrong. I couldn't figure out what happened. I dressed well. I sat straight in my seat. I didn't talk to anyone. I smiled at her. I was alert, and I knew the material. What was wrong? She never said a thing to me the rest of the period but went on with assigning the class a unit test for the following day.

That night, after supper, I puzzled over those looks and the stare Mrs. Kaiser gave me in class for no apparent reason. I felt angry, but I didn't understand why. What was the matter with her? I did everything correctly, and she still acted upset with me. I wondered if I would ever understand teachers. Probably, she thought I was too slow to be in her special class. I reread the entire unit that night, which was something I never did. I even read a few extra chapters because they were interesting. I spent all evening preparing for that unit test. I went to bed early, so I would have plenty of rest to tackle her intimidation the next morning. I ate a good breakfast, which I knew would give me enough endurance to persevere through her class.

When I took the test, I was calm. I answered the last question before anyone else did. I looked around the room and was surprised how much time was left in the class period. The other students were still struggling with the last few questions. I forced myself not to turn in my paper first. I stayed in my seat and reviewed every question one more time. I took the full period and turned in the paper two minutes before the bell rang. On purpose, I was the last person to lay my test on Mrs. Kaiser's desk. As she held my test, I looked her in the eyes and smiled. She noticed that. Her eyes met mine, and I grew more confident because I could see her puzzlement.

She asked, "Is there anything wrong, David?"

"No, Mrs. Kaiser. I thought this was a most interesting group of chapters we studied in the last few weeks. I wish the entire book and this class could be this informative about why humans do what they do." She stared at me without saying anything.

The day following the test Mrs. Kaiser passed out the graded exams. She returned my paper last and mentioned that I received the highest grade of all. Without raising her voice, she looked at me and said, "I never thought anyone would score this highly on my difficult test. Certainly, I never thought it would be you, David. Well! Well!"

I thought she smiled. It appeared that she did not know how to handle the situation, so she dropped her eyes, turned her back to me and the class, and we started working on the next unit.

This nearly negative reinforcement did have a positive effect on me. I knew that I made an impression on her. I was interested in the subject and tried to do my best. When I decided to study hard for the exam, I was surprised that the material flowed through my eyes, effortlessly, because my interest pulled the pages through my mind. This was one of the few times in any classroom when I felt completely relaxed. I found myself studying psychology for the simple interest of learning, not to achieve a grade, or to impress the teacher.

Unconsciously, I discovered synchronicity. This surge of energy occurred when I studied the topic simply for my own enjoyment. I now know that I waste my time if I do not find myself absorbed in the message of what I am doing. This is the only way I overcome my fear of failing and achieve my potential. Thanks to Mrs. Kaiser and those students in my class, I now see my potential reflected more completely when I blissfully enjoy my work.

8

My Journal, My Child

"Books are . . . engines of change,
windows on the world,
'lighthouses' erected in the sea of time."

–Barbara Tuchman

A person's writing may develop into many things. My attempts at creative writing take the form of a journal, a personal warehouse of ideas and feelings. These bits and pieces expand into larger ideas or are used to support other thoughts that come later. My journal began as a skinny, empty, three-ring notebook and evolved into a robust creation with a personality of its own.

My first attempts to originate something from a non-artistic life, bound in the past to mediocrity, surprised me. Without a conscious effort on my part, this unassuming notebook began eating pages scribbled with pathetic sentences, mostly unconnected, didactic, and plain. A few pages held feeble attempts at poetry. They were stilted, forced rhyming patterns on the most boring topics, and some hid scattered, embarrassing attempts at describing the passions of a midlife crisis or two.

Without knowing what I was seeing, the birth of a journal took place before my eyes. The thing increased its appetite. From a page a week, it soon demanded a page every couple of days. As it got bigger, it enjoyed eating more. It wanted to be fed daily, then ten or twelve times a week. What began as a puny, scrawny creature developed muscles and a healthy attitude towards survival. Each time its covers opened to consume more pages, I sensed the bellows of lungs expanding, as though it aggressively inhaled new life.

With increased bulk between the covers, its lips pushed wider apart. It began to smile at me, as it sat on the shelf across the room. I imagined it standing up and strutting in front of those other notebooks that kicked sand in its face when it was just a little child. Now that it has become aware of its own mortality, it insists on the four basic health groups for good writing: literature, vocabulary, rhetoric, and composition.

Like a parent, I am learning a lot about myself by watching my new child at play, and I think I see the time coming shortly when I will have to find it a name. What would other people think if I did not have a name for my new baby? When it begins to talk, will it develop a psychological problem stemming from a lack of self-confidence without an identity of its own?

Nicholas Notebook? Julia Journal? Danny Diary? Bradley Biography? Ashley Album? Pilar Page? Elizabeth Exposition? Imogene Imagination? Karma Klassic? Big Bubba Book?

At times, I think my journal is a goldfish in a bowl, swimming around in circles without much room to explore or opportunity to develop, while others watch from a position outside my goldfish vision and feel pity for my writing inadequacy. Often, I feel clumsy like Godzilla smashing Tokyo. Of course, some pages show me to be nothing but a large mouth bass looking for a sucker's hook. Other pages convince me that I am a lazy dog waiting in the sun for that creative idea to come by, as I continue to slumber in ignorance.

In rare moments, my little friend also convinces me that I am a rose bush with the softest petals, and I celebrate my uniqueness. My back arches proudly when the pages open to something worth reading a second time. It is an auxillary backbone, which supports me when times are tough. Now, my journal, the teacher, explains to me inner ideas that are hard to discuss with others. It acts as a prism, reflecting the lights of shadowy, mental images. It sings the blues to me in a rhythm I can understand. It is both masculine and feminine. It is a collection of inspirations that make me a whole person. It is a growing tidal wave. It shows me doorways between the pages that appear unexpectedly. It carries me to places new and old. The binders reach out and hug me, when I need it the most. It is portable and reinforcing. It is a friendship, a crutch, a magic carpet, and a time machine. Alternating between a snail and a 747, its speed constantly fluctuates between short scribbles and long flashes of lightning.

I help shape my destiny by learning to vary the sentences I use. Life speaks for itself, but I listen with my journal. Each written page is a brush stroke added to my life's painting. Page after page, I view myself in greater depth. One day, I am a bird trapped in a small cage. The next, I am an eagle soaring close to the face of the Mysterious One.

9

My Room

"There is no frigate like a book
To take us lands away,
Nor any coursers like a page
Of prancing poetry.

This traverse may the poorest take
Without oppress of toll;
How frugal is the chariot
That bears a human soul!"

-Emily Dickinson

I respect Emily Dickinson as much as any writer I ever read. She is precise and direct. Reading another's book does the above, but how wonderful it is to achieve these aims by writing one's own words. My journal mirrors my mental room, who I am, and what I think, in the same way my private room reflects my physical being.

When ideas come my way, I don't get discouraged. I trap the thoughts between the covers of my notebook. When I organize my journal, it is neater, and so is my mind, much the same way as organizing my personal space does. I am as imaginative as I want to be. To know my room is to understand me.

Randy Travis sings "Oh, What a Time to Be Me" in the background, and the ceiling shakes from two children running upstairs. The country and western tune coming from the radio reminds me of my roots. My head may be in the city, but my heart is still in a wide-open, country hayfield.

The calendar on the wall knows time divided by twelve. I read it now just as in my youth, when I read the cloud shapes in the blue sky, while I rested between wagon loads in the hayfield on hot, summer days.

41

This basement room is cluttered and full, a warehouse of ideas and dreams. There is an incomplete project in each corner. The cedar chest cradles half-written letters. The file cabinet stores my history: bills, school papers, magazines, and folders. The chipped wooden desk anchors my sanity and keeps me from drifting away into a chaotic world.

My room collects the scattered parts of me. Larger than the pockets of my pants when I was a boy, these four walls provide the same service, a repository for treasure gathered on numerous adventures. My room talks to me, like my typewriter, an old friend and a past hero that is too dear to give up. Now, it is used only to address envelopes, since it gave way to its brother, "Big Mac," a stronger, faster, cleaner, word arranger. They are two great loves of my life.

They talk to me like Dad's favorite horse, Gin, talked to him. That marvelous, chocolate, Morgan, four-footed lady who lived to be thirty-five years old and only died because she fell on ice in the pasture one winter and couldn't stand up again. She was the one who made him feel like Tom Mix every time he rode in a parade. He fed her first before the other animals on the farm. She was the one who carried him as fast as the wind, even though Dad's feet and back still held shrapnel he collected in France during World War II.

Pictures of my father stand in one corner of my room, the ones of him at basic training in 1941 at Camp Robinson, Arkansas, with his buddies from the 134th Nebraska Regiment, Company B, where he looks so young and is just a kid himself. There is the memorial case that holds his Army patches and medals, including the Bronze Star and three Purple Hearts. Beside it are other items I remember when I think of him: a copy of the letter General Eisenhower sent to all servicemen at the beginning of the Allied Expeditionary Force's Great Crusade and the Normandy Invasion on D-Day, a Charter Member Certificate from The Board of Directors of The Battle of Normandy Museum (Omaha Beach), a letter President Clinton sent to the families of deceased veterans, and the flag given to me by the Honor Guard when they removed it from his casket at the graveside after a moving, military funeral.

My father's favorite painting, a smiling John Wayne, hangs on the wall with these personal memories. Wayne is wearing a cowboy hat and boots with a rifle slung over his right shoulder indicating everything is all right, now.

On the bulletin board, Nolan Ryan stares at me and says, "The only one who can tell you you can't is you. And you don't have to listen." H. D. Thoreau never leaves this room. My drummer beats my tune and is never far away. Gandhi whispers the seven worst sins: "Wealth without work, pleasure without conscience, knowledge without character, commerce without morality, science without humanity, worship without sacrifice, and politics without principle."

I keep a 1944 Kodak Brownie photograph of Grandfather Schock in my desk. A giant of a man, as I remember him, he had the largest hands and fingers of any male adult I ever knew. His strength came from farming before tractors, and those hands husked large fields of corn without benefit of machines. They wrapped themselves around my heart every time I saw him.

Such a physical person was a rare thing for me to see as I grew up, but the softness of his touch and the warmth of his smile taught me that muscles and compassion can coexist in the same male body. I learned much from his example. To this day, when I think of a positive, male, role model, I think of him. He walked quietly and confidently like he knew what would happen every minute. He wasted nothing, not even time. When he wasn't in the fields working with the soil or his animals, he was reading.

The only things larger than his arms and hands were his principles. These fond memories of my mother's father make me think of Robert Kennedy's words: "Each time a man stands up for an ideal, or acts to improve the lot of others, or strikes out against injustice, he sends forth a tiny ripple of hope, and crossing each other from a million different centers of energy and daring those ripples build a current which can sweep down the mightiest walls of oppression and resistance."

My son's school trophies and ribbons hang on one wall, until he chooses to take them down. His picture of The Hulk, once his childhood idol, doesn't scare him anymore. He turned into his own personalized Lou Ferrigno. His first pen pal was a Japanese girl who lived in Tokyo. Her picture remains on the board. Pictures of forests and mountains captured his attention many years ago, and he lives to climb and ski them. As a supervisor of a ski lift at a major Colorado resort, he brings his dream to reality every day, when he goes to work.

"So little time, so many books." The remaining space in my room, which is not taken up with pictures, mementos, and computer items, is covered with books. The shelves sag. The more I read, the more I discover I know next to nothing at all.

The more books I consume, the more my vision changes. My eyesight demands a new pair of glasses every two years with a more intense prescription. My vision grows toward myopia. Now, I see less and less of the horizon, but I focus more and more on what is close to home inside me. I am still a child who wants to find truth and searches for wisdom and love, only to find out how very small I am.

I have lived in this house for thirty-six years and spent more time in this room than any of the others. My room prods me, talks to me, and points the way. I need to listen more attentively to what it says, like I would with any good friend, and I need to spend more time with me.

10

Nurturing the Writer's Garden

"A book must be an ice-axe
to break the seas frozen inside our soul."

–Franz Kafka

This year I tried to make something special happen in my classroom. I decided to teach what I knew was right for me and my students. I sacrificed the tired, traditional composition format of grammar, mechanics, and the five-paragraph theme. I instituted a new divine trinity: the first person pronoun, writing from direct experience, and the journal. My high school is an above average, college prep school. The faculty and administrators are very happy with the school's image and success. It provides good teachers and a good education for the average, above average, and the gifted teenagers. I saw a way I could add to this quality by increasing the warmth and humanness in English class. I offered a place of caring for the individual student with personal journaling.

So far, I do not regret my decision. In fact, I see tremendous improvement in my students. In previous years, I taught the following levels of English composition: pre-remedial, remedial, hospital English, terminal English, pre-civilized sophomores, academic juniors, twelfth grade night school, creative writing, and college undergraduates (freshman and advanced upperclassmen). Many students from each level told me in secret, so none of their friends would hear, that they felt writing to be fun, again. They told me they learned self-discovery through their writing.

I was most inspired, however, to find proper punctuation magically appearing where necessary, when the students believed that what they were writing was important and that someone was going to read and believe what was written, inside and outside the classroom. Passion entered into their papers to stay, to grow, like seeds well-nurtured in a garden.

In my high school classes, one day a week is devoted to journal activities. By far, the most successful writing-teaching technique I have used is the incorporation of the personal journal into all of my lessons. I feel so strongly that my students' writing is improved by journaling that 20% of my class time is concentrated on this yearly project.

I have prepared a list of over 300 topics for students to write about if they cannot find interesting ones of their own, but I always give them a choice of topics on which to write. The ones who can't think of something to write about must find new excuses not to write.

On the first day of class, students design their own coat of arms by cutting out graphics from old magazines to pictorially represent the following personal characteristics: 1) one important item of their past, 2) one important item of the present, 3) one important item of their future, 4) one important item of how others see them, 5) one important animal that symbolizes their personality, 6-7) two favorite quotations which illustrate important concepts with which they identify.

Each student must bring a loose-leaf, three-ring notebook with rings two to three inches in diameter. I store these binders in my classroom, so they are available, and I read them at my convenience during the day. The students take loose-leaf paper home with them, and when their assignments are finished the next day, they simply insert the pages into their notebooks in class. This prevents the loss of homework and increases orderliness.

I read every notebook weekly. Each student's writing is titled which lets me read selectively when I must, but each page is read. I leave a check on each page to let the students realize their pages have been read, even if I don't comment on each one.

When it comes time for grading the journals, I inform the writers that the grading is done by the pound. Effort and quantity are the primary qualities I am looking for. I only make positive comments in their journals to reward students for their efforts.

This writer's garden receives only nurturing and fertilizer, never any poison or salt. With this system, I have seen complete changes in students' attitudes toward English class within two weeks. This positive reinforcement of the writer's individual communication greatly affects not only my classes but the students' self-confidence and their outlooks on life in general.

This year-long project develops into a warehouse of feelings, emotions, ideas, and personal revelations. It surprises me every year how many students tell me, "Mr. M., it is now spring, and I was re-reading my journal last night, but I don't feel the same way today that I did last September." The students' ideas move and evolve because of their writing, and they are aware of their own growth.

Frequently, I give students a topic and only four minutes time to finish writing their ideas. Usually, they will write one-half page per four minutes. In a forty minute period, an average student will finish four to five pages. This is half of their weekly writing assignment for the journal. I give "A's" to those who produce ten pages a week.

I try not to let the students come up for air on these days. Just as they start to breathe easily, I give them another topic. I always let them leave room on their paper, as much as they want, so they can go back and finish any uncompleted thoughts when they relax. In this way, they can finish as much as they choose and add to what they started in class. Jokingly, I say to switch hands, if their first one gets tired while writing. Even the slow composition students enjoy the challenge after a few times, because they make so much progress in their journals. The journal is our biggest project undertaken all year. Neatness, effort, pride of ownership, creativity, they all count, but quantity is paramount. Some journals are all letters; some are all short stories; some are all possible mixtures. I don't care, as long as they write. All prose papers written in class or for class may count.

Creativity is encouraged daily; we write at football games, at museums, in study hall, even looking out windows. At the end of the semester, 150 pages are required for an "A." All other grades are pro-rated on a percentage basis.

Extra credit may be earned in excess of 100%. I have given journal grades as high as 300%. If the students want to write, I never put a ceiling on their productivity or their earning potential. Write on. Right on.

I write every assignment that I give my classes, as though I was just another student. Sometimes, I read my work out loud to the classes and show my rough draft errors, too. I treat all the students as if they were in my small group. This practice breaks barriers more easily than any other strategies I have used, when it comes to getting reluctant student writers to share their work in class. My own children keep journals, and sometimes, I bring their work to share with my students.

One student of mine graduated a few years ago and continues to write. Her journal now includes thousands of pages. Once every two months, she brings her notebooks to me, so I can read them.

After clearing the trip with her parents, this student and I went to a local cemetery one day, so she could say important words to her grandmother whom she never had a chance to speak with before her favorite relative's death. The student's invitation to accompany her on this special journey was the most unusual one I have ever received. We found the grave and sat down in silence. One hour in the cemetery with this student was a guaranteed stimulus for writing. She has not quit writing in her journal since.

I try to have fun with the journals in many ways. I include stickers with funny sayings on them. "Far out!" "Now you are going to town!" "Excellent!" "Teeeerrrriiiiiffffiiiicccc!" The stickers remind some of elementary school, but when a student of mine does not get one, I sure hear about it.

The students stopped complaining about how much writing they were doing after the first quarter, when they saw that I was not going to stop expecting them to produce, and neither was I going to quit writing myself.

When they saw that I was passing out grades in excess of 100%, they became believers. If a student writes more than ten pages per week, I liberally pass out extra credit grades, give resounding praise for any student's enthusiastic compositions, and send the best writings to the *Fine Lines* editors, recommending them for publication.

Journaling is the greatest tool that I have found for encouraging students at all levels to write, to improve their writing, and to enjoy writing. No matter how slow students might be at the beginning of class, if they don't give up on writing, I promise I won't give up on them. No matter how good students might be upon entering the class, if they continue to write in their journals, I promise them they will improve.

I tell all of my students that if they keep faith in their journals, their notebooks will keep faith in them. Writers must write what they mean and mean what they write. Write on. Happy journaling, and keep the faith.

11

Simplicity, Synthesis, Synchronicity

"We lie the loudest when we lie to ourselves."

-Eric Hoffer

"We must be true inside, true to ourselves,
before we can know a truth that is outside us."

-Thomas Merton

I am responsible for my actions and my thoughts, and I want to learn much more than I now know. I sense the knowledge inside of me is much more important than the external knowledge I could acquire. No one else can teach me what I need to know. My insight comes from life experiences, and I must teach myself how to see.

Every year, I teach *The Scarlet Letter* to my eleventh grade high school students and renew my interest in the Puritans who settled New England. My mother traces her family name (Steele) to Abigail Adams in the United States and to Charles II in England. The Puritan religion played havoc with her family tree. On my father's side, Charles Martin was, in fact, the treasurer on board the Mayflower when it docked at Plymouth Rock. We can't say for certain if he was one of our family ancestors, but it is possible.

The Puritan custom of labeling people into two groups was one of their interesting habits. If these people believed in the need to reform the Church of England and tell citizens the "pure" interpretation of the Bible, they were "saints." If some expressed any doubt in the strict Puritan philosophy, obviously, those people were "sinners." Life was so black and white, so simple. "Saints" and "Sinners," that is all there were.

King James I threatened the Puritans when they asked him to change ceremonies carried into the Anglican Church from the Roman

Catholic Church. He said, "I will make them conform, or I will harry them out of the land." He demanded a simple life, too. Subjects had to follow his way and conform, or they had two options: go to jail or leave the country.

These Puritan farmers, merchants, professionals, and scholars, especially from the University of Cambridge, came to be regarded as gloomy fanatics. For example, "They objected to bear baiting, not because of the pain to the bear, but because of the pleasure to the spectators."

Some teachers try to "harry . . . out of the land" students who feel a need for new ways of thinking about old problems. These teachers feel they are on the front line of ethical values, and to alter their nineteenth century views is the same as succumbing to modernism. Many of their students feel no sense of unity and no sense of inner awareness. These conservative teachers take so much pride in being orthodox, like King James, that they retard many learning processes.

Rush Limbaugh sends his newsletter to interested subscribers for $20/year, but he "charges $10 more to liberals." Doctrinal instructors put that "$10 more tax" on creative and non-traditional students in the way of stress, pressure, and a "saints or sinners" approach to education.

Opportunities to learn arise when different points of view appear on the scene. The greatest single lesson I learned in education revolved around the definition of the word "synthesis." The main point of view in any discussion is called a thesis. The opposite point of view is the antithesis. Many hard life experiences taught me that seldom is the truth ever in one of these two opposing points of view. Almost always, the truth is somewhere in between the thesis and the antithesis. The truth is in a blending of the two, the synthesis. Once I accepted this lesson of life, I learned what tolerance really meant.

When I learned that my ego determined my thesis or my antithesis and what I thought I saw was based on my pride in knowing the truth, I understood what Joseph Campbell meant when he talked about the "dragons" in our world.

Campbell's discussion of the mythology surrounding the European dragon in literature and religion points out to me how important my ego becomes in determining what I think I see in any situation. European dragons are negative barriers our egos place in front of us to prevent us from achieving our desires and goals. Writer's block is one dragon, which I must deal with on a regular basis, and my own ego creates it, not anyone else. Thus, I learned to slay my dragon.

This specialist in comparative mythology changed my life. He taught me the importance of following my bliss and why I should expect synchronicity in my life. He taught me to look inside myself to find the life force to which I am connected and trust that my reason for living will become known. He showed me why, when I do what I am supposed to do with my life, synchronicity will "open 1,000 doors."

Campbell's many books and forty years of studying cross-cultural mythology reinforced what I sensed in my childhood: most major religions have more commonalities than differences. If we study them far enough and rise spiritually high enough, somewhere beyond this mortal plane, they come together as one. That intersecting point is not located outside us. It is only reached through an inward journey.

When my father was a young man, he was dressed in full combat gear, ready to board a troop ship to cross the English Channel and do his part during the Normandy Invasion in June 1944. I remember seeing newsreels of General Eisenhower talking to young men, just like my dad, the day before they left for their meeting with "Hell on Earth."

"Ike" asked one soldier if he had a religion. The smiling paratrooper said, "Yes, sir!" The general said, "Good. Where you are going, you will need one. It does not make any difference what it is. It just matters that you have one." I wonder if this awareness is not just as true now, as we face our personal "Normandy Invasions," today.

A recent retiree became interested in construction of an addition to a shopping mall. Observing the activity regularly, he was especially impressed by the conscientious operator of a large piece of equipment. The construction worker went beyond what would have normally been required and reached for excellence in all he did. The day finally came when the retiree had a chance to tell the man how much he enjoyed watching his scrupulous work. With an astonished look on his face, the operator replied, "You are not the supervisor?"

Most people need supervisors looking over their shoulders to ensure excellence. Many look at the way we live our lives and draw conclusions about our self-reliance. True students have few supervisors looking over their shoulders. I see good students remaining disciplined, because they are courageous enough to become their own supervisors. They do not need someone else telling them how to study or when to read. Sincere students, teachers, and managers sow their visions of simplicity, synthesis, and synchronicity to students, employees, and peers.

12

True Wisdom

"There are thousands of thoughts lying within a man
that he does not know 'til he takes up the pen and writes."

–William Makepeace Thackeray

Anyone who writes knows chaos is necessary for creation.
If ideas are worth learning, they are worth writing any way possible.
Form follows content. Let truth come out any way it can. Its looks will
be secondary to the message. In Genesis, when the world was formed,
chaos was necessary. It is one thing to be busy, but more importantly,
we must know what we are busy about. True wisdom knows what to
overlook.

American motorists spend six months during their lives waiting
for red lights to turn green. If we face a pause in our creative life, let's
imagine we are at a red light like a motorist and do something useful
until the light changes. What could we do? Notice the beautiful leaves
on the trees next to the curb? Recognize how marvelous the children
look going to school? Remember their scrubbed faces? Imitate their
happiness? Good writers use the time they aren't writing to experience
life around them, store glimpses of clarity in their sentences, and
warehouse ideas for later in their journals when the composition muse
reappears.

On January 28, 1887, giant snowflakes fell on the Coleman
Ranch at Fort Keogh, Montana. They were 15 inches across and 8 inches
long. We know every snowflake is different; no two are alike, not even
the 15" x 8" ones. How can a microscopic snowflake see the same world
that a huge one does? Everyone's view of life is different, but does that
mean we don't all come from the same source? All writers must take
confidence in the fact that their life experiences are valuable resources
on which to draw their ideas. Every human being is a metaphorical
snowflake.

Leonardo da Vinci could draw with one hand and write with the other, at the same time. Do I dare think I see the world the same as he did? No, of course not; however, I am confident that much of what I know of the world is worth sharing with others.

I remember thinking it was absurd to imagine eating food or drinking liquids unaided, under water, in the ocean. Human beings must follow certain physical laws. Eating underwater was for fish not people. Then I took a scuba diving class. Not only did I learn how to eat bananas and other food under water, 30 feet below the surface, but I progressed to drinking pop out of a bottle without drowning, when I removed my mouthpiece. Now, when someone tells me that a flamingo can eat only when its head is upside down, I understand, but humans survive because they adjust. As a species, flexibility is our primary attribute.

Beauty justifies art. To say, "I like it," is enough. Baudelaire felt, "All is order and beauty." I know what he meant, but I am not sure I agree with him. Things in life that are ordered and pretty are usually dependable and pleasant. We arrange our existence around their order, and we rely on their lack of irritation. However, communism was ordered, and some thought its principles were beautiful. I support democracy fervently, yet I agree part of it is extremely chaotic. Much of it is not ordered, and a large part of it is not very beautiful. By choice, I wouldn't live anywhere but in a democracy, so I question Baudelaire.

Miles Davis, one of the world's best jazz trumpet players, liked to say, "There are no mistakes." In writing, I believe this, too. Write on. Don't erase and edit until the creating is done; just write, write, write, and write. One can always edit at the end. It is more important to create than to edit. Fueling the imagination is the most important part of the writing process.

Thomas Last Fuller said, "Seeing is believing, but feeling is the truth." My writing is a snapshot of who I am today. I may change tomorrow. As I search for the real me, I feel my words, and they give me courage to go on. This is a small place in my life where I take off my mask and do not worry about someone saying, "Trick or Treat." Here I am, a "sojourner," a seeker of truth, as I find it.

Like Randy Travis said in his song, *Be a Point of Light*: "Stand up tall and do what's right/There are many heroes we never know/There are dreamers making dreams come true/There is nothing you can't do/ One by one points of light are calling out/They're a ray of hope in the darkest night/If you see what's wrong/ and you try to make it right/you will be a point of light."

A writer's vision is a solitary, lonely, challenging, haunting, passionate, misunderstood, and gnawing business. It is a cruel tyrant beyond rational comprehension, with mystical beginnings. It is a sleeping germ in dormant seeds, agonizing, groping, and stumbling for meaning. Defying the odds, a few writers grow, and their love of the language creates rainbows after human storms. These writers speak from the heart about what they know and learn from personal experience. They open windows, expand hearts, grow souls, and focus minds. "Better keep yourself clean and bright; you are the window through which you must see the world" (George Bernard Shaw).

Most writers suffer from a lack of courage that keeps them from trying to develop their craft. Real artists work, not to become famous, but because they must. Writers must write words, practice their art, purge their souls, and know what they think by putting ideas into print. To write and fail is a learning experience. Not to try is to lose. "Not failure, but low aim is crime" (James Russell Lowell, American editor).

The mirror of our lives is our work, not others' work but our own. Out of the jungle build a path. Out of despair create a purpose. Out of youth develop maturity. Out of barriers find transcendence. Out of yarn knit a sweater. Out of paint draw a picture. Out of a death in spirit breathe a new beginning. Out of ordinary walls build a picture window. During the Holocaust of World War II, those who kept minds and hearts active were windows of hope to the others who could not think beyond their pain. A writer writing well is like Siddhartha listening to the river.

Walls are barriers. They limit expansion and access. Some walls, which are built to last forever unbreached, keep ideas and dreams beyond my reach. Those who say walls are necessary because the world is still a dangerous place seek their progress in the making of more bricks to lengthen and heighten the status quo. Many walls are political hurdles created by opponents of change who continue to stress yesterday's dragons instead of dealing with today's realities.

I am not who I once was. My old problems are gone. New ones await solutions. I can't keep one foot in the past if I want to realize tomorrow. Tearing down walls takes so much time and strength. I waste myself with the annihilation process. It is thrifty to pierce the walls and build windows in some, doors in others.

13

Writing a Window

"You have to read in order to write . . . art is a seamless web,
and we all latch into it where we find a loose end."

–Archibald MacLeish

I love windows. I love their beauty, their simplicity, and their view. They provide protection from the cold. Their light pierces the dark. They give hope to the confined. Windows symbolize so many things to me, and they help make me whole. How I remember these windows is how I think of my past. How I feel about these windows is how I see my future.

For many, life is a bleak, passionless existence. I see lives of boredom all around me. Barriers of all kinds, real and imagined, keep people from participating in active, productive lives. Blank stares, uncreative minds, and empty hearts reflect this lack of direction and purpose.

Windows are miracles of glass, silica, and heat. They protect us and provide decoration in our world. They allow us to dream in safety. Windows frame what we see and limit our vision. They outline our view of the world. If windows are metaphors for our lives, they come in all shapes and sizes: tall ones, skinny ones, short ones, some stronger than others, some easily broken, old ones, and new ones with many different levels of tolerance.

Windows show character and variety, just as an individual's personality does. Windows come in many shapes and sizes. Their diversity reflects their uniqueness. A simple window symbolizes a simple life. Beveled glass windows allow the sun to reflect through prisms creating rainbows on the floor and walls, visual kaleidoscopes produced by nature.

Stained-glass windows do not allow people inside a room to look outside, but they let the sunlight teach stories by reflecting images from the glass. These beautiful spectacles of art, nature, and philosophy provide inspiration hundreds of years after their construction.

A room with windows is a room that breathes. Windows become metaphors for transmitting images of hope, vision, and energy. They allow us to examine all aspects of our lives by focusing our attention on specific developments.

Clear windows show those with nothing to hide. Cloudy, dirty windows mirror confused and unpolished individuals. Shaded windows prevent others from viewing inside. People, in the same way, shade themselves by remaining closed to others, inhibited, and do not see the light.

Where windows are placed in a building affects their appearance. In Nebraska, windows placed on the north side of a home may receive less punishment from Mother Nature. Southern windows are tortured by the sun's rays and the strong winds from the southwest all year long. While north windows remain smooth and clear, the sun's radiation on the south side forces the glass to expand and damages them.

Mirrors are windows coated on one side. They reflect backward what they see. Certain people are like mirrors. They reflect backward and use none of their energy to perceive the visions in front of them.

Like the masks we wear during the day to conceal our feelings, window shades allow different amounts of sunlight to enter our rooms. When we are depressed, we pull down our shades. When we feel happy, our shades let in more sun.

If the eyes are the windows of the soul, a person's view can be influenced by the thoughts and feelings allowed to penetrate those windows. A glass of water may be either half-full or half-empty depending on a person's point of view. Positive windows may simply be clean ones. Negative windows reflect life's dirty smudges.

Windows hold anything a person's mind imagines. "If dreams were for sale, what would you buy today?" Unlimited possibilities present themselves to some; others, whose creativity is poverty-stricken, limit themselves to the common. For some, windows only hold items of the past; some see only the present; a selected few reach into the future. Many people use their windows to see inside their hearts and outward into the world.

Writing can become a metaphorical window. This process allows writers to describe what they feel after writing words on paper that best illustrate their specific emotions. Readers see through the window frame that writers create, and together both envision the same picture, emotion, and thought.

"Nothing great in the world has been accomplished without passion" (Friedrich Hegel, German philosopher, 1770-1831). A wonderful quotation like this one becomes a window of wisdom that travels the ages. What a wonderful window we look through, when we learn to read.

In an Eskimo language, the word "to make poetry" is the word "breathe." Poetry is an important window, and it allows us to breathe fresh air and see farther into the world.

Like pages of glimpsed clarity, a panoply of window panes makes me aware of sunshine, clouds, and unlimited possibilities available in life. I built a sunroom in my home and am surrounded by windows. I see the birds in the sky, the stars at night, and a rainbow of colors each day.

Each window fine tunes my day and adds increased focus to my life. An occasional cracked glass or a little dirt in the corner affects the vision I achieve out of each respective one. Each window becomes a frame of mind, a frame of hope, an opening of my dreams.

Handshakes, books, connecting the "1,000 points of light," five fingers turned into a fist, nets made from a single strand are all windows of meaning. These images provide different cultural lenses, blazing insights through which we teach ourselves from our own life experiences. These windows of perception show the way to the other side.

As dogs are said to resemble their masters in looks and temperament, windows in homes reflect the personalities of the owners. A window's appearance shows the owner's concern, attitude, and imagination. Owners who take the time to keep their windows clean enhance their ability to see the world around them more clearly.

One of the largest windows of my life is my work. Out of the day's chaos, this window brings order. In the educational forest, I build a path. Often confronted with student despair, I create purpose. Surrounded by youthful discontent, I search for maturity. Enveloped by teenage barriers, I imagine transcendence. Given yarn, I knit a sweater. Shown colors, I draw a picture. To escape a death of spirit, I breathe a new beginning. Surrounded by four ordinary walls, I imagine a picture window. As I grow, the view from these windows becomes more focused.

14

Five Years of *Fine Lines*

"There is something in our minds like sunshine
and the weather, which is not under our control.
When I write, the best things come to me
from I know not where."

-G. C. Lichtenberg

The fifth consecutive year of our *Fine Lines* publication ended with the year 1996. The first issue was only four pages long and took five months to produce, but it allowed students an opportunity to show others outside the classroom the results of their clear thinking and proper written expression. The last issue, forty-eight pages of fiction, non-fiction, and poetry was written for people of all ages who wanted to improve their writing skills. What started out as a classroom-newsletter project turned quickly into a quarterly journal with a twenty state membership list.

Fine Lines looks forward to the next five years with enthusiasm because it now receives creative writing, prose articles of medium length, and poetry from students in schools all over the nation and adults of all ages and occupations. Last year, *Fine Lines* printed a poem from an eighty-three-year-old grandmother, the work of doctors, lawyers, scientists, educators, and janitors. *Fine Lines* accepts submissions from anyone regardless of age, vocation, and education. Submissions came from as far away as Japan, Denmark, and Switzerland. Authors simply need the desire to write, share their conscientious efforts with others, and remember Horace's words. "He who has hit upon a subject suited to his powers will never fail to find eloquent words and lucid arrangement."

In the gray, cold, short days following the winter solstice, when many people celebrate the end of one year and the beginning of another, when the pain and suffering of last year is more memorable than the anticipation and hopefulness of the new, clean slate of 365 days to come, it is easy to focus on what went wrong in the recent past than what went right.

Let's choose to leave behind the mistakes and errors we made last year. Don't bring them into the New Year. Instead, let's remember the blessings and wisdom we experienced during the Earth's last trip around the sun and meditate on how to use those things to make this year even more productive than last year.

Looking back at the progress of *Fine Lines*, I feel the loss of not just another year but five years. Not twelve months passed like lightning, but sixty. Where did they go? I can't help wondering what I should remember from everything I felt and witnessed during this time. What did I learn? Am I wiser now than at this time last year or five years ago?

This passage of time highlighted for me more of who I am. Writing through the last five years, I felt much like a prospector digging in the ground for nuggets of gold. Alone, like any prospector must be to find his veins of precious metal, a writer endures the silence to hear his internal messages, pushes over the next hill, and tries once more to be in the right place at the right time. Often, I wrote up steep mountains in vain. I followed valleys to dead ends. I thought what I found was of worth at first, only to realize I had nothing but "fool's gold." Eventually, I located a few pieces worthy to be taken to the assayer's office. Knowing that one's treasure is another's trash, I share below the maxims I gathered over the last five years while publishing *Fine Lines*, and I thank our membership for their constant support of this quarterly journal.

- Play my tunes slowly, simply, and sincerely.
- Passion in life is necessary to be happy.
- Without my family, the dike would collapse.
- Routine kills my spirit.
- Friends are family extensions.
- Knowledge fatigues.
- Wisdom rejuvenates.
- We have only begun to learn what we need to know.
- I was raised outside the prison of prejudice.
- Heresy is necessary to increase knowledge.
- The greatest battles of life are internal.
- Doing is less fulfilling than creating the dream.
- Artistry and beauty are done well in any job.
- Homes are empty without books.
- Hugs keep us healthy, and silence expands our souls.

- Teach. Don't preach.
- We live better when we expect to die.
- All that goes around is not merry.
- I hope to sing all my songs before I go.
- The less people speak, the more they listen.
- Joy is not in things; it is in us.
- The greatest travel distances are not geographic.
- Remove your head and come to your senses.
- Our worst fault is to hit the nail on the head too hard.
- Go slowly. Go far.
- There is no finish line.
- It is better to be the poem than the poet.
- Pain is necessary for growth and change.
- Trust and faith we all can sow.
- We know infinity when we become what we see.
- Let's write as though our lives depend on it. They do.
- Truth needs a soldier.
- Dreams are the children of the unconscious.
- We must write on.

15

Mother's Day and the New Woman

"Use words that soak up life."

– Virginia Woolf

Mother's Day celebrates the hard fought victories all mothers have won. In their often quiet ways, mothers who struggle for freedom and equality have been taken for granted too frequently. It is unfortunate that we do not think of their sacrifices more often than we do.

Mother's Day would not be if it were not for Anna Jarvis, the woman who suggested in 1917 that this nation celebrate its mothers. She did not have any children herself. Maybe, that is why people listened to her. Her idea was not self-serving. She deserves more recognition than she received, but I feel that women in general, deserve more recognition than they receive.

Many male attitudes towards women of this century were developed during the 1800s when the French philosopher, Rousseau, influenced people with his ideas on the nature of humankind. He was explicit in his attitude towards women in this passage from *Emile*, a novel about the development of a young man: "She is to be brought up as man's subordinate, to minister to his needs, and to give him pleasure." This attitude was shared by the average Frenchman of this time and later reflected in the art style that was popular in the late nineteenth century in France called Art Nouveau. Later, this style influenced much of the western world.

Napoleon Bonaparte influenced the attitudes of the French people and the Art Nouveau artists in the nineteenth century when he instituted the Code of Napoleon, which reinforced the male domination of women. This code states: " . . . a woman should obey her husband, that a father has sole authority over his children, and that a woman can not go to law without her husband's consent." Women were little more than property.

The Industrial Revolution improved economics and changed women's place in society. They became more involved in politics, worked outside the home, and began the women's rights movements. In England, Parliament debated the suffrage issue eighteen times from 1867 to 1905. In this country between 1870 and 1910, women ran 480 campaigns in 33 states trying to put women's suffrage before male voters.

The pneumatic tire was instrumental in women gaining the right to vote. With the bicycle, women had an effective vehicle for transportation and were not so dependent upon men. In order to ride bicycles, women wore less restrictive clothing. "Bloomers," the divided skirt, came into existence. Amelia Bloomer wore this new style in spite of the criticism she received, because she felt it was comfortable and becoming to her when she jumped rope or went to classes. Still, it took a lot of courage to wear them in fashionable circles, when her father was a Congressman in Washington, D.C.

As women's roles changed, men began to feel threatened. They increased sexual taboos, so the fear of women became stronger. Women were put onto pedestals and praised from a distance. The men were safer, but the women became helpless, harmless, and no longer a threat to insecure masculinity.

The Art Nouveau style that dominated the male attitudes toward women for so long really was an escapist style of art and tried to capture the "perfect woman." This style was trying to say that the only real power for women was through their femininity and refinement. Without their femininity, women were nothing. As history clearly proved, femininity was not a source of power at all. The only real power women could have was the power they fought to get through independence and equal rights.

Women were portrayed as paradoxes, beauty and evolving life on the one hand and evil and the source of original sin on the other. Too often, women were painted as either the good "Virgin Mary" or the wicked "Scarlet Woman." This whole period of art comes towards the end of a long century of Victorian repression. The artwork done in that period reflects the hidden neuroses of the artists who were men, of course.

David Martin

Alphonse Mucha was the most characteristic artist of this period. He was obsessed with hair and with women as sexual objects. He is the artist who did most of the Sarah Bernhardt posters that portrayed her with long hair curving around her body. She became the "Mucha Woman." He felt in real life that women were like his posters, decorative objects. He once told his son, "Woman was, for him, not a body, but beauty in matter and acting through matter." In other words, Mucha saw women themselves as empty, shallow creatures, whose only virtue was the fact that they could portray beauty.

In many ways, these artists who captured the imagination of much of the world and affected the attitudes of men and women in this country created a falsehood that lasted to this day. They could not accept the changing woman and went overboard on one last hedonistic fling, just as the women's rights movement started, just as women were chaining themselves to public buildings and recognizing their own individuality. As the Art Nouveau style faded into the sunset, the preoccupation of the female as a decorative object and the last ditch, anxiety-ridden attempt to keep women in their traditional places slipped from sight. Out of these ashes came matriarchs like Susan B. Anthony, Elizabeth Cady Stanton, and Lucretia Mott, their Herculean efforts brought respectability to all women.

One day in a little town, Elizabeth Stanton was talking when a man started mocking her and insinuating about the women's duty to increase the race. He said, "My wife has presented me with eight beautiful children. Isn't that better life-work than exercising the right of suffrage?" She carefully inspected him and then remarked, "I have met few men in my life worth repeating eight times." Stanton was a work horse for what she believed. In one campaign, she gave 1,600 speeches for only 28,000 votes. Many of lesser character would question her effectiveness.

Theodore Parker spoke in the Music Hall in Boston, regarding his position on what he felt was the most momentous question of the day and of his generation. The topic was the public function of women. He was a troublemaker and ahead of his time, which meant that he disturbed people when he said things like: "The domestic function of woman, as a housekeeper, wife and mother, does not exhaust her powers. Woman's function, like charity, begins at home; then like charity . . . goes everywhere . . . to make one

64

half of the human race consume all their energies in the functions of housekeeper, wife and mother, is a waste of the most precious material that God ever made . . . woman has the same natural rights as a man . . . I do not see how I can shut myself into political privileges and shut women out, and do both in the name of inalienable rights."

Parker went on to say in this talk that women in general have a better heart, a truer intuition of what is right, and a stronger sense of the beautiful and the Holy. He felt the excellence of men and women should be united if humanity was to reach its fullest potential. The highest development of the human race will only be achieved when women are recognized as the peer of men, not only at the fireside but in all the meeting places of the nation. This old suffrage song sung to the tune of "America" gives a loud and clear message supporting these points of view:

> "My country 'tis of thee
> To make your women free
> This is our plea
> High have our hopes been raised
> With these enlightened days
> That for her justice praised
> Our land might be.
>
> My native country thee
> Grant us equality!
> Then we shall see
> In this fair land of light
> Justice and truth and right
> Ruling, instead of might
> Trust liberty!"

Let us hope we do not have to fight any of the old battles between the sexes. May the SCUM (Society for Cutting Up Men) and WITCH (Women's International Terrorist Conspiracy from Hell) groups forever rest in peace. Someday, sayings like "From the doll house to the White House!" and "Shirley Chisholm, here we come!" will be archaic and unnecessary.

Mothers, please, teach your sons that just because the status quo relationships between the sexes were good enough for their fathers, those relationships can improve during your children's lifetime.

This Mother's Day, buy your son a copy of the *Women's Liberation Game*, or start with the books your son is reading. Buy books that do not have the girls always playing with dolls, keeping house, and jumping rope. Get books that show girls as more than "sugar and spice and everything nice." Why can't girls climb trees, collect worms, and the boys learn to cook?

Did you hear about the group in England that is rewriting *Snow White and the Seven Dwarfs*? They thought no self-respecting girl should have to wash dishes for seven men. Snow White still bites the poisoned apple and passes out, but this time the hunter saves her life, because he hates to see all that intellectual potential wasted. Mom, our sons are not just oppressors, if they are allowed to continue the old stereotypes; they are fellow victims along with our daughters.

Do you know what Elizabeth Cady Stanton did to the Bible? She was a religious skeptic and eventually rejected all religious authority. She created her *Women's Bible*, an audacious and outrageous act of independence. It was not a piece of scholarship, but it was an attack on the Christian Bible as a source of the condemnation of women. She said, "The chief obstacle in the way of woman's elevation today is the degrading position assigned her in the religion of all countries . . . an after thought in creation, the origin of sin, cursed by God, marriage for her a condition of servitude, maternity a degradation. Such is her position in the Bible and religion." She advocated abolitionism, gentle rationalism, not taking the Bible literally, offering prayers to the "Mother and Father God," individualism and self-esteem for all people, male and female.

As Stanton approached her seventy-fifth birthday, she was weak with years of struggle. Her 240 pounds slowed her down, but she refused to stop her combat. She worked on an autobiography, gave speeches, lobbied for the Women's Suffrage Amendment, spent the winter of 1889 in Omaha, Nebraska, with her daughter, Margaret Lawrence, and did not become sedate or respectable. After an argument with Lucy Stone, Stanton wrote to a friend: "The men and women who have been battling for freedom in this country are as grand and noble as any that have ever walked the earth. So, we will forget their faults and love them for their many virtues."

Many mothers have done much for the freedom of both sexes and the quality of life for us all. I hope my son and daughters grow up knowing of the valuable contributions to the United States these women made: Olympia Brown (first female preacher), Sophia Lyon Fahs (women's rights), Margaret Sanger (birth control), Mary Wollstonecraft (*Frankenstein*), Dorthea Dix (mental institutions), Julia Ward Howe ("The Battle Hymn of the Republic"), Mary A. Livermore (Sanitary Commission), Elizabeth Palmer Peabody (kindergarten), Clara Barton (Red Cross), and Louisa May Alcott, Margaret Fuller, and Catharine Sedgewick (literary figures).

This Mother's Day, let's promise one another that our sons and daughters will grow up knowing that at birth there is a bonding of the child with both the mother and the father, that children have a masculine and feminine side to their characters, a dual nature that allows boys to be sensitive and girls to show a masculine side of their personality. Well-rounded human beings will show this dual nature and not suppress one part of themselves.

Mothers, celebrate your being today. You deserve it! Help your sons and daughters to realize their full potential. Show us the peace, healing, and creative qualities you possess and much of the world is lacking today, so we may become like you.

Happy Mother's Day!

16

A Night at the Symphony

"When the bright angel dominates, out comes a great work of art,
a Michelangelo *David* or a Beethoven symphony."

–Madeleine L'Engle

Discordant sounds from the instruments on stage filtered through
the concert hall. The musicians bent toward their music in focused
concentration, tuning responsibly, listening intently for any note out of
pitch, and all the while keeping a watchful eye on the assistant conductor
for his signal to ready themselves for the conductor's approach. The
house lights dimmed, and a few latecomers hurried through the lobby
toward their seats.

A sudden hush of voices followed by applause told me the
maestro had positioned himself in front of the orchestra. Handel's
"Vivace" from Sonata in B Minor lavishly filled the air, as the doors
silently closed. The filtered music washed over me, as I noticed
one person did not return to her seat in time to hear the second half
performance.

The bartender seemed puzzled why the two of us stayed
at separate tables, unhurried and alone. He fussed and cleaned the
countertop loudly, trying to move us out.

I continued to sip slowly my glass of champagne. I refused to
be rushed. I always sit alone at the same table during intermission and
watch the others, the highbrows and the social climbers, talk about
themselves and their importance; however, I distance myself from them
emotionally.

I attend the symphony, because I appreciate skill applied to
discipline. When people achieve perfection in any field, music included,
I am interested. I notice the underdog. I protect those who wish to
improve themselves. I admire the struggle, the pain, the work involved
to raise oneself to a higher place. To build visions of truth in a dark hall,
to use a language without words, to place musical notes in the proper

sequence, to move people to tears, to create a mood with a bow and strings, all these reasons inspire me to return.

At each performance, I imagine the peace and quiet of the concert hall transformed to the outside world. The evening's musical meditation becomes a slice of heaven, an oasis of culture in a desert storm of work and drudgery. In the background, I could hear the beginning of Rachmaninoff's "Prelude in C Sharp Minor."

The other person still sitting at her table was a stunningly attractive woman. She looked at me casually with warmth and polite assuredness. When she noticed me looking at her, she walked directly over to my table and sat down without a word spoken. Her direct manner, her expensive clothes, and her model's figure made me gulp for additional air. She asked for a double Manhattan Sweet on the rocks. She drank it in three swallows, laid the glass silently down on the table, and asked for another.

I could tell the bartender assumed we were together. I never saw this woman before that night, but I continue to see her still. Her long, black hair hung to the middle of her back. Her skin was a creamy, light brown, possibly Indian, Native American, or Hispanic. Her full-length, Siberian, silver fox coat almost touched the floor and accentuated her loveliness.

We looked at one another because there was no one else in the room besides the bartender, and we were both tired of looking at him. For a minute, neither of us spoke.

"Nice performance!" I said, at last.

"Very," she replied.

"Lose your seat?" I smiled.

"I got here late from another engagement. I am not as quick as I use to be, and I don't like to ask people to move when the lights go down. That's such an inconvenience, don't you think?"

"Well, maybe, but I doubt if most people would mind if you passed in front of them."

"You are kind. I can listen to the music just fine right here with you. Are you a musician?"

"I seek the music of the soul, but that is the only instrument I know. The music inside the hall is beautiful, but their notes are different than mine. Come here often?"

"Whenever I can get away from my other obligations, I come to the symphony, but it is not nearly often enough," she said.

She looked toward the doorway, as a strange man came inside, leaned against the wall, and stared at me from the other side of the room. He moved his gaze around the room slowly. He couldn't hear us talk, but he returned his attention to me, frequently. His animal alertness intrigued me. His vigilance offset my lethargy. I decided he was a concert security guard, then I ordered another glass of champagne.

She saw me look at the stranger, then brought me back to our conversation. "What do you enjoy about the symphony?" she puzzled.

"I like, want, need some time to myself, where I can think and reduce my stress. Sometimes, my work gets to be too much, and you?"

She replied, "Well, I can't find enough time in my life to rest. There is so little chance to sort out my life. I heal myself by listening to classical music. I wonder, sometimes, if there is enough substance to my existence, so I come here. If I am lucky, I find a little more reason for living, then I go home."

She crossed her legs and let the long fur coat fall off her shoulders. "No family?" she asked and smiled.

"Not now," I answered.

"Are you alone?" she said.

"I am now," I was forced to admit. "You?"

"Don't ask. My happiness is manufactured. I am not what I seem. Life is so unsure, isn't it?" she continued.

"With each day, I learn how unsure it is," I said.

Solemnly, she looked into her glass, then at the man at the door, and back to me.

"I was forced to depend on myself at an early age. I found I had to desire something in life to keep my soul alive. I learned to ask for what I wanted, or I never got anything important. I had to believe what I wanted would happen for me, or events and people passed me by. I discovered if I asked and believed enough, I got my share of life. Unconsciously, I learned to take charge of what I did, anyway I could. I didn't expect the world to come to me. I knocked. I asked. I believed. I received. Life happened."

"What did you ask for?" I said.

She smiled and slowly pushed her hair back on the side. "I asked for attention, affection, and security, in that order."

I said, "What is wrong with that? Everyone asks for those

things."

"Yes, I know, but I didn't ask for enough from life. I settled too cheaply. I found through many men and experiences, that if I believe in myself and leap in the direction of my dreams, a net appears under me and collects me when I fall. That hasn't happened much, but what I regret is that I didn't leap more often in the direction of my dreams."

As Bach's "Siciliano from Sonata in E-Flat Major" played background music for us, she poured out her views of life and how she took the short cut to fame and fortune. I wondered why she wanted me to know this.

Where is her husband, her boyfriend? Somebody close to her should be hearing this, not me. An intimate acquaintance should hold her now. It is not right to spill this precious substance of one's life in front of a stranger.

She turned to me, offered her hand, smiled, looked a little embarrassed, and said with slightly slurred speech, "Trust me. I may be nothing to you, but I learned many things in my life. There is nothing I am more sure of than this. Listen to your heart, first and last. Money does not matter in things that are truly important. We have it all when we love ourselves and each other. Life is meant to be enjoyed. Work is part of the equation, but the work comes so we can be happy and satisfied. We must learn to follow what makes our heart happy, and then we will find life's meaning."

I looked at her. She was so beautiful, and she seemed so intelligent. I could feel my mouth open in stunned amazement. I tried to talk, but only garbled words came out. As I fumbled to say something equally profound, the security guard walked over to our table and spoke directly to her in a hushed and official tone.

"Madame, the Senator is now here. He is in the car outside and is waiting for you. Please follow me. He is in a hurry and must leave at once. You will come, now."

She grimaced slightly, as she looked at the table, then her watch. When her eyes raised and met mine, I could see tears. Then, her expression appeared to be one of a tired warrior who must fight one more battle but would rather be some place else. She pulled herself out of her chair, fussed with her coat, and sighed loudly. Without looking at me or saying good-bye, she arched her back, straightened her shoulders, turned, and walked straight for the revolving glass door. Abruptly, she

71

stopped and turned to look back at me.

"Take the time, dear, to find yourself first, before someone else finds you. If you don't, you won't be able to do what you want with your life. If you fail to leap when you have the chance, that other person may put a fence around you, so you won't be able to follow your bliss in life. Even if the intentions are well-meant, the barriers we place around ourselves become prisons, just the same."

Then, she turned on her heels and walked through the door into the night.

17

A Personal Affirmation

"You are, when all is done,
just what you are.
Put on the most elaborate curly wig.
Mount learned stilts
to make yourself look big.
You still will be
the creature that you are."

-Johann Wolfgang von Goethe, 1749-1832

Writing an affirmation is hard work for those who want to become writers. They are often filled with self-doubt, if not self-loathing. Affirming ourselves as writers takes serious effort. To maintain what we believe to be true, honest, and sincere writing depletes us of energy and strength. No matter how we pretend to be other than what we are, writers are at their best when they show the world their true natures. Good writers learn through life experiences what they know and how much they have yet to learn.

I discovered my love for reading in my maternal grandparents' home. My mother's father farmed and worked hard, like most farmers do; however, he read every thing he could find, when he wasn't on the tractor, milking cows, or mending fences. Grandmother worked hard also, and she read whenever she sat down.

Reading material was located throughout their two-story farmhouse. It was easily accessible to me, even though I was a child. I turned the pages to see how they felt in my hands and read until I realized the articles were much too advanced for my young mind. Then, I laid them down, but I felt more adult each time.

Every book, magazine, and newspaper became a magic carpet, a wonderful experience, a tunnel to the future or the past, and a time machine. My grandparents' library transported me from the dark, rich soil of Nebraska to the moon, to the nation's Capitol, to Roy Rogers' ranch, to the Rose Bowl, to Wrigley Field. Reading took me anywhere I wanted to go and to many places I never dreamed were possible. Once I learned to love books, writing my own words became the next step.

"Uncle" Bill Schock was another positive male role model as I grew up. He was happy, ebullient, intelligent, athletic, knowledgeable, a leader but reserved in nature, a bomber pilot during WWII, a college graduate, and a friend in my youth. As the editor of the *Falls City Journal* newspaper, he showed me what power there is in the written word. His writing changed people's lives.

With his editorials and investigative articles, he helped our small town thrive, remain together when it argued over controversial issues, learn from its mistakes, and grow. A life-long resident of Falls City, he became the town's favorite spokesman. The way he lived his life showed me what it takes to become a good man in this world.

When I became a paperboy in the fifth grade, I learned how important newspapers are for educated citizens in this country. I hurried to the paper office each day after school, so my customers wouldn't receive their papers late. I remember reading each day's edition, from the front page to the last, before I got home for supper. I began to understand why many countries place reading and journalists in such high regard. When I learned about Thomas Jefferson's ideas regarding educated citizens and how they protected this country's democracy simply by reading and becoming self-educated, I vowed before reaching junior high school that I would read at least one newspaper a day as long as I lived. I continue to keep that promise; however, sometimes, it is now two or three papers a day.

What if we aren't inspired, if we don't have words at our command, if "writer's block" has its grip around our throats, our hearts, and our souls? Do we raise the white flag, find another job, and surrender? Do we say to ourselves, "I can't do this. I can't write any more. I can't."

If we succumb to negativism, we will not write, and we will not deserve to be called writers. Good writers don't say, "I can't." They often say, "I don't know much about this topic, but I will find out. I may not have what I need to write something at the moment, but I will work on it until I find enough to write about later."

W. Somerset Maugham said, "Only a mediocre writer is always

at his best." This tells me there is always room for improvement. With each rewrite, I hope to improve my work, and after many years, I learned the following lessons about writing and life.

- Good writers write daily.
- Creative flow stops quickly when the writer's ego arrives.
- "Writer's block" is an excuse for not being oneself.
- Writing the impossible is one way to grow.
- What needs to be written changes daily.
- Writers have no proof of thinking until a first draft appears.
- Writers' important personal journeys are not geographic.
- Writing well combines caring, information, and passion.
- Writers must hear the language beyond words.
- Good writers are not static.

I don't talk much, but I read and write, because I can't imagine living without words. My wife and two daughters use more words before 10 a.m. than I do all day long. They are gifted oral communicators. Compared to them, I feel inadequate, but words still are beautiful and necessary to me. I am slow to speak, because I choose to think first, before I react. I want to communicate correctly the first time, not apologize for an error later. Writing is an intimate form of communication, and I value the process of stringing words together in order to form concise thoughts, which precisely illustrate who I am and what I think, without using "wigs" or "stilts."

18

First, a Dream

"In dreams begins responsibility."

-William Butler Yeats

Some of my high school English classes were concentration camps of pain. The boring grammar and punctuation drills seemed to never end, and I felt my case of "senioritis" was terminal.

One day, my teacher methodically reviewed Shakespeare's writing, again. To protect myself, I entered "dreamland." Right then, she stopped talking and asked me a question about one of the bard's sonnets the class just finished reading.

I felt embarrassed, because I could not answer the direct question. I did not know or care what page we were on in the text, and I resented her intrusion into my reverie. I planned to build my own "epiphany" by myself.

The other students laughed vigorously, but I saw a calmness and peace in her eyes that made me feel warm inside. She was sincere. She knew my mind was somewhere else important and let me go back there.

I would have paid more attention if she looked like Gwyneth Paltrow in *Shakespeare in Love*, but she didn't. This grandmotherish-looking teacher smiled and said with all the tenderness in her heart, "That's all right, David, dreaming is allowed in English class."

Her show of support and trust in me as an individual remains after all these years. I loved her for that simple act. She believed in me. I felt she understood the importance of sudden insight and the rarity of intuitive understanding.

I owned my seat in that class. My voice was heard. I belonged in that room. I had freedom and presence. It was a safe place. It was a strong place. I could bring my fragile dreams into her classroom and share them with this adult who knew where I hid my heart.

I regret I never told her any of this before she died. Somehow,

I think she sensed my feelings. It was years later when I brought this memory to my consciousness, dealt with it, and put those emotions into words.

If anything happens in life, first there must be a dream. We are a "dream deprived" people. We don't dream enough because we don't see enough. To be truly happy and successful, our dreams must come true.

Creative people revolt against the world, as they see it, and develop a world of their dreams. They revolt to find a principle of existence. These are metaphysical revolts, people against the conditions of life, aspirations toward clarity and unity of thought. Artists in any field explore their souls, try to discover who and what they are, create meaning out of chaos, and search for their own inner compasses. Joseph Campbell said happiness comes from recognizing one's soul and following one's bliss.

"To thine own self be true, then as night follows day, though canst be false to any man" (Polonius, *Hamlet*). This is life's mission and the purest form of love. It equates into spiritual growth, courage, irreplaceable character, and the strongest bond imaginable.

What we emotionally feel is more important than what we physically sense. Newton's Third Law of Motion states that every action has an equal and opposite reaction. Theologically, this translates into Karma and The Golden Rule. Intention causes effect. Angry people draw angry people. Hell is not a place where we are assigned. It is a place of our own choosing.

We spend our lives seeking our fate. Where we were born, what station in life we entered the world, what gifts we have now - none of these things prevent us from crossing paths with our destiny. We work hard not to hear messages sent to us in life, and we ignore signs in our dreams which show us the way to our future.

If my dreams could come true, I would write of wisdom and how to succeed in life. I would tell about the steps I must take to maximize the opportunity given to me at birth, the chance to taste happiness and experience a few raptures on my journey. I would illuminate the occasions when mankind becomes entirely alive. I would remember to look into the void of space on the darkest night of the year and see the brightest lights in the sky.

Like Curly (Jack Palance) in *City Slickers*, I would look for that "one thing" in life, the one thing that makes a difference, our reason for living. Our choice won't work for anyone else, and no one can tell us what our one thing is, but our dreams will.

My daughter, as an eighth grader, dreamed of finding anyway possible to reach home plate and score runs for her softball team. Returning from practice one day, she said: "Dad, I know you'd like to know you aren't the oldest father of an eighth grader at our school anymore. A new student entered our class today, and her dad is older than you are. He doesn't have any hair at all." Dreams are egotistical, too.

Another time, after babysitting all evening for the two boys next door on New Year's Eve, she came home at 11:00 p.m., feeling very mature and authoritarian. She saw Mom and Dad watching television and eating popcorn, waiting for the ball to drop in Times Square to signal the start of another year.

She said, "What's going on here? Where is the party? Are you two dreaming? Get up, Dad. I want to dance."

She dragged me out of my chair in the living room and onto the kitchen floor. We danced for twenty minutes, until I was laughing so hard tears ran down my cheek. She tore off a green leaf from one of the indoor plants, held it over my head, and yelled, "Mistletoe!" so I would kiss her on the cheek. We twirled and hugged. When she was done, I knew this year would be filled with wonder and many more dreams.

I hope to find a "Doctor of Dreams," a healer to those with hidden scars acquired from the well-fought wars of life, one who breathes hope into the lost and malcontent, one who provides energy for broken hearts and puts wind beneath their wings.

This dream doctor would carry me to the unknown and back, over the bridges of understanding. I would become a professional pilgrim. Travelers learn the most by telling their own stories, and I would become observant, then tell my own tales.

With my dreams, I invent myself. I sense a new vision that allows me to see through the fog of life. I observe a new dose of reality that documents the pain but is also a healthy vitamin. I learn to dream, create, and heal.

"Imagination is more important than information."

-Albert Einstein, 1879-1955

19

From Pain to Purpose

"Writing is the only thing. When I do it, I don't feel
I should be doing something else."

-Gloria Steinem

Motivation is moving towards a goal. Abraham Maslow,
the famous psychologist, said there were two kinds of motivation:
deficiency motivation, changing an unsatisfactory situation, and being
motivation, seeking a positive goal after lower order needs are met.
People may use writing to achieve either one.

Writers often build armor around their psyches by using words
to overcome inferiority, deficiency motivation. They add layers of
protection and self-esteem to inner feelings of inadequacy and learn
to compete with no one but themselves. What they write is personal.
Fear, shyness, inferiority, and inadequacy rise into the open on the
writer's own terms, in safety and confidentiality. Writers construct
strong foundations with words to support their needs. A firm outer
image develops through the writing process, because the inner image
is patched and repaired, which is being motivation. Journal writers
develop healthy egos. Formal writing, to prove ourselves to others,
to be accepted, and to receive better grades are not the reasons one
usually writes in a personal notebook. However, some of this writing
might develop into a product one could turn in for a school assignment,
because an intellectual component surfaces.

Journal writing wants to penetrate the flab, the insincere, and
the lies of life. With the proper attitude, it touches unacknowledged
feelings, becomes character completion, attitude development, and a
healing form of expression, not just for the classroom but for life. It
involves self-study, life education, skill, effort, a positive attitude, and
discipline.

Personal writing may require increased introversion, a change in value systems, and a movement toward self-realization. It reduces one's ego and increases the development of creativity. It ties the unconscious to the conscious.

Albert Einstein said, "The most beautiful thing we can experience is the mysterious. It is the source of all true art and science." Writing gives us a tool for probing the mysterious, the unknown in our unconscious and connects it to our awareness.

Being awake in all aspects of life teaches us that we do not know as much about ourselves as we think. Intensive journaling shows us there is more to explore than people previously thought, and one of the best ways to do this is to write about our dream images which illustrate psychological archetypes from our collective unconscious. Dreams restore emotional balance by igniting spontaneous creations on which the writer builds.

Carl Jung, the founder of analytical psychology, used the term "archetypes," which are psychic structures that organize and hold material in our unconscious file folders during our dreams and reveal important ideas about ourselves. Intuitive writing is one effective way to touch these deep seated psychological structures. Journal writers often find shadows in their writing, the archetypes coming to life. When people face the sun, most do not see their shadows: those dark sides of their natures, their weaknesses, those parts of their being in need of repair. Shadows seldom surface in our conscious life, but when we touch our unconscious, we often reach those areas, which need the most work. Turning our backs to the sun allows us to see the shadows we forgot were behind us. We limit our own development by continuously looking into the light.

The best writers recognize their shadows, accept them, and confront the biggest shadow of all, the inflated ego, the largest barrier in our path, the fire-breathing dragon called perfectionism. Writing empties the mind of distractions and offers glimpses of emotional clarity. Affirmations positively written transform normal awareness and increase one's serenity. Journals write the dragons away and provide opportunities to visualize one's goals for the day, for the year, and for life.

Writing success involves conserving energy, plugging leaks, and increasing one's vision. We see with our eyes. We hear with our ears. We touch with our hands. We taste with our tongues. We smell with our noses, but we understand with our hearts, and open hearts make better writers.

People find strength in the careful selection of their language. Many go from pain to purpose. There is nothing like a serious writer's block to discover what true opportunities are in the next paragraph. There is nothing like a crisis to reveal a true epiphany. We create our own miracles. The rhythm of life and the spirit of the universe are at our fingertips. Writing is a state of mind and reduces life's negative influences. Accentuate the positive. Practice. Practice.

Confusing aspects of life make us feel that we go around in circles. When we drift, become discouraged, depressed, lonely, alienated, and bored, stringing words together becomes a silent place to record our confessions. Often, if we take the time to write about our difficulties, we see spirals instead of circles. Spirals indicate that even though we continue to go around, we may move upwards at the same time. This is progress, even though it is cyclical. Writing for a few minutes daily can change people's lives. Serious writers learn in a short time to find road signs for their lives. They write their way down the Yellow Brick Road, to Oz, and home again.

Writing is stress therapy for the gridlocked, an adventure of the mind and heart. One cannot stay depressed and continue to write a journal. People become optimistic, if they write enough. Write On!

20

In Search of Soul

"Science without religion is lame.
Religion without science is blind."

-Albert Einstein

Early in my life, I learned to respect "sojourners," seekers of truth. I felt I wanted to be one, but it didn't take me long to figure out I would be alone on my journey. I didn't find many others willing to make the necessary sacrifices to discover truth and wisdom. Truth was where I found it. It came in different sized packages: small and large, plain and colorful. Wisdom was how I applied that truth. I was often naïve, because I assumed the study of religion was the study of truth.

The French author, Voltaire, said, "He who seeks truth should be of no country." No country or religion has a hold on "the truth." As a child, I considered that was why so many preachers moved a lot. They had no country. They had no home, because they looked for spiritual truth which has no borders.

I sensed a lot of emotions early in my life that I submerged into my unconscious, because I wasn't prepared to handle them. I didn't know how to put them into words. I was young, yet I had insightful flashes of realization. I was not a prophet. I didn't want to be. I was not a savior. I didn't want to be.

Even then, so long ago, I knew many tough questions, but I could tell wisdom seldom came from having right answers. Truth appeared when the right questions were asked. I believed the proper currency of developing wisdom was learning to ask the right questions. What perplexed me the most, as a child, was when I found right answers before I discovered the right questions. I always was introverted, not shy, just quiet, reserved, and thoughtful. Consequently, this confused my parents.

Silence is a friend of mine. I discovered spirituality alone, before I was ten years old, listening to my inner voice in isolation, watching the trees bend in the wind at my grandfather's farm in Nebraska. I found a reservoir of wisdom ready for me to grasp when I developed my intuitional skills. I sensed a purpose to life in the silent world inside me. At the same time, I puzzled over my cosmic ignorance and the great mysteries of existence.

Peter Drucker said, "The most important thing in communication is to hear what isn't being said." I learned to listen more to the stillness of stars at night, the mute sun's rays at dawn, and the hushed breathing of the ones I loved. I began to turn up the silence.

I resorted to a "Desiderata" - Bobby McFerrin attitude when my perplexities became overwhelming: "Life is unfolding as it should," and "Don't worry. Be happy."

Later in life, I learned not to trust people, especially ministers who said they had all the truth I needed. They said I didn't have to think anymore for myself, because they would do that for me. Studying history closely taught me to beware of Trojan horses of truth. My ability to choose is my best gift in life, a symbol of my freedom, one I will not give away to anyone else, no matter how hard I have to work to keep it.

We are the salvation of one another. Although I could not find the right words to say what I felt before I was ten years old, I asked enough questions to sense that if I followed my bliss in life and combined it with enough suffering (hard work), I would be successful (the right doors would open) in a way I still did not understand. Today, I would call that Faith + Action = Salvation. In much the same way a child jumps from a moving swing to see how far he can land away from the starting point on the playground, our respective "leaps of faith" require an adventurous spirit, leaving the comfortable behind, and trusting we won't arrive back on the ground in a bloody mess.

George Bernard Shaw said, "Better keep yourself clean and bright; you are the window through which you must see the world." Keeping our personal temples clean is a symbol of individual responsibility. When more sand in the hourglass has escaped in our lives, the clearer it is to see into our souls.

As a child, I read a lot about Thomas Jefferson. He said, "To love God with all thy heart and thy neighbor as thyself is the sum of religion." I wondered if that couldn't be the core of the religion I was

looking for. I had even more encouragement when I read Jefferson's
Bible, the one where he cut away all the words in the King James
Version that could not be attributed to Jesus Christ. He felt the words
of Jesus were among the most sublime he ever read, but the rest of the
Bible was written by men and could be tossed. They were just words that
followed priestly and political structures.

When I realized for every seven people in the world, one person
eats with a knife, fork, and spoon; two people eat with chopsticks, and
four people eat with their fingers only, how could one religion ever reach
a whole world with such diverse living conditions? If we all live under
the same sky but have different horizons, how will our souls connect?

One day while I was looking at the horizon and the setting
sun, I considered God and how He created the world. I wondered if He
worked liked many city crews I observe while driving around town these
days, where four men watch and one person does the work. What if
the universe was created this way? What if four watching gods decided
to pitch in and help one working god? Is our world the product of one
working god, or did they all help?

What if our world was created while the God Mayor of the
Universe was in Reno on vacation, and the City Council God decided to
take matters into his own hands, settle the labor strikes himself, and get
things created once and for all? This approach probably works in some
universes.

It was an accident when I learned the words "buddha," "rabbi,"
"priest," "minister," and "professor," were all a form of "teacher." Could
there be a lesson here? Real seekers might simply be looking for a
leader, one who knows the right ways of living. I discovered early in life
when the student is ready, the teacher will come.

Recently, I was vacuuming the basement, and my dog was
helping me. She is loyal to a fault. I cleaned, and she barked, trying to
warn me against the loud, evil "snake-like" contraption I was moving
over the floor. Obediently, she followed me around the house, like a
trusted servant. Religions salivate to have members act like my dog. I
thought about her soul. Then I thought about changing her name from
"dog" to "god."

I imagined two fleas on my dog arguing about which one of
them was in charge, as the dog was barking loudly at my vacuum cleaner
which she had no way of understanding as long as she lived. How

similar is this imaginary scene to the one I see happen when two people argue about the "rightness" of one religion over another? Like two fleas on my dog assuming they had control over the hairy, four-footed animal, people argue over their understanding of God. I imagine this divine awareness leaning down, laughing mightily at the humans as they argue.

On my life's journey, I stopped studying religions and began studying my soul. I don't study anyone else's soul. I just study my own. I like people, philosophy, and religion well enough. It's churches that bother me. Individuals put up with me when I talk in metaphors, which is my natural way of conceptualizing experience. Churches ask me to use creeds and dogma to explain myself. I believe in the power of stories, like *Peter Pan* and *The Truman Show*.

Great visions start with small dreams. Tinker Bell told Peter Pan he could always find her in the real world and speed back to "Neverland" by looking for her somewhere between "Sleep" and "Awake." In other words, we can find the vision of our fantasies, as we are coming out of sleep and entering the waking process. Scientists tell us this is the period of our unconsciousness when we recall our nightly dreams. It is also our most creative period. Salvador Dali forced himself to wake up after falling asleep, so he could paint the images in his unconscious state. We would do well to remember more of our dreams.

The Truman Show script is a creative masterpiece. The movie's theme applies to all of us. We must take the boat we are given at birth and sail on our journey of life the best we can, not depending on others to live our lives for us. We must set our own horizons and fight our own battles. Life is more than a TV show. We must not become a nation of couch potatoes, viewing the lives of others. The action generated by a TV producer and director is not the substance of our lives. A person's real religion appears in one's personal experiences. We are born with all we need, and we must live the rest of our lives to bring it to our consciousness.

I always loved words, and in grade school, I puzzled my parents by asking them why we used the words we did to communicate. I couldn't understand why no one else questioned why "red" was red, "mom" was mom, and "English" was English. I learned words have meaning because we say they do. We believe in their definitions. That's all. There is no mystery to it, really. Religions work that way, too.

The word "poet" in the Greek language, where it originated, meant a creator, someone who developed anything from nothing. A poet, then, could mean a cabinet-maker, a homebuilder, and a person who constructed chariots. Later the word "poet" was isolated to mean a person who creates written expressions of emotion and feeling. As *The Truman Show* illustrates, we must become our own poets and create the poetry of our lives.

I learned to sum up my religious experience in one word, "awe." When I look at the night sky, I am "awe-struck." When each of my children was born, I was filled with "awe." Is religion anything more?

Wilhelm Roentgen's discovery of the X-ray helped the medical world immensely. However, many devoutly hoped this discovery would let us see the human soul. I feel there is a world beyond this one, and I am able to reach it with my dreams. Pain and pleasure, success and sorrow form our soul, and we shouldn't be in such a hurry to rid ourselves of the pain. While we need to understand and enjoy the experiences that bring us happiness, we also need to understand and "luxuriate in" our unhappiness. A life lived soulfully is not without its moments of darkness and foolishness. I may not find it with X-rays, but I will search for my individual soul as a source of divinity.

"The most beautiful things in the world cannot be seen or even touched. They must be felt with the heart" (Helen Keller). The mind is truly a secondary organ.

There is talent. There is skill. There is genius. There are dreams. There are spirits. Each one of us has a soul, but do we know how to find it, explore it, and develop it? A person can exist forty days without food, twelve days without sleep, six days without water, and five minutes without oxygen, but how long can we live without knowing who we are?

After years of searching for my soul, the following truths became important for me. I will be curious to the end. For every thesis, there is an antithesis, and the truth is in the synthesis. There is passion, rapture, bliss, and epiphany in ordinary life. The soul has an unlimited capacity to grow.

Tell stories. Our lives are the books we are writing. They possess wisdom.

Love, beauty, and truth are the trinity for any artist, and they are spelled in many different ways.

Silence matters. Simple is best. Gratitude is genius.

Peace in the world begins with peace in my world. I can't be the person I am meant to be when I am angry. Live each day to make a difference. Don't just be good. Be good for something.

21

Just a Man

"Life is no 'brief candle' to me. It is a sort of splendid torch
which I have got hold of for a moment, and I want to make it burn
as brightly as possible before handing it on to future generations."

-George Bernard Shaw

My father died July 31, 1994. He refused surgery and
chemotherapy treatment for his lung cancer. After his quadruple by-pass
heart surgery a few years before, he swore he would never go to another
hospital for an operation, and he didn't. He chose to "ride the bug out."

My father's life was one battle after another, and his World War
II experience captured the rest of his life. Even though he lived to be
seventy-six years old, his army combat in the European Theater changed
him forever. His work, marriage, family, and children revolved around
the memories he brought home from that war violence. For the rest of
his life, he endured its physical and emotional scars.

Dad was not a great man by society's standards. He was just
a man like so many others who risked their lives to make the world a
better place for all of us by ensuring our freedom from tyranny. Usually,
he kept his emotions and memories locked up inside himself, but once
in awhile, I could dislodge some information he kept from the rest of the
family. He would begin telling me a small story of his experiences, but
before he finished, he always caught himself, remembered that he was
talking to a child, got emotionally upset, and walked out of the house. I
was a kid then, and he felt I wouldn't understand what he went through
during those times.

The most significant events of his life were those horrible
days during the war. I remember Dad telling me the story of General
Miltonberger, the Commanding Officer of the WWII Nebraska Division,
feeding him and other soldiers a nice meal then talking all of them out
of trying to join the paratroopers, because he needed them in his ranks.

They stayed in the 134th Infantry Division until the end of the war. Dad and his buddies were good soldiers, and they did their duty.

Dad told me about meeting Jack Dempsey in the fighter's New York City restaurant the night before the troops sailed for England. Dempsey was surprised that he and a friend, two small-town Nebraska boys, went so far out of their way to find his restaurant and meet him that the ex-boxer bought them dinner. Because of this late night adventure, the two were officially AWOL, but the Company Commander was glad to see them when they returned in time to sail on the troop ship, and all was forgiven.

In World War II, the soldier death ratio was 1 in 48 US soldiers; in Vietnam, it was 1 in 1,113 and in the Gulf War, 1 in 2,667. The basic difference in these ratios was the advanced medical help and rescue methods that transported the injured from the battlefield to medical hospitals. General Eisenhower had 91 Allied divisions to defeat the Germans, 60 of them American. Of the 4,454,061 US soldiers who embarked for Europe and Africa, 3,604 were lost at sea. In the first four months after the Normandy Invasion, Germany suffered 800,000 casualties.

During his service, Dad received half a dozen different combat wounds, three Purple Hearts, and an 80% disability rating upon returning home. He came back to the states carrying pieces of shrapnel the doctors would not remove from his back, because they were so close to his spine. The worst injury took place in liberating St. Lo, France, after D-Day. He was struck by mortar fire and couldn't move. Medics placed him on a stretcher and tried to get him off the battlefield. He thought he would never make it to safety, because there were so many bullets flying through the air.

He was sent to England where he was hospitalized. Soon, the Army thought he was healed enough to return to duty. He became a company runner, delivering messages to units up and down the frontline, and German snipers shot at him. One day, while returning to headquarters, he saw three soldiers kneeling beside a wounded, screaming, American, who was writhing on the side of the road. A doctor amputated the wounded man's leg to save his life. There was no morphine present to aid the soldier.

"The Battle of the Bulge" in the Ardennes Forest was a desperate thrust Hitler threw at the Allies. Of the 600,000 Americans involved, 80,987 became causalities. About 19,000 were killed, and 15,000 were captured. Some 47,000 were wounded. Gen. George Patton's 3rd Army rescued them. Dad was attached to Patton's group, and he told me many stories about fighting during the winter there.

Louis Rhodd, a Native American friend from Rulo, one night crouched in an artillery shell crater. Dad jumped into the same crater for safety. There was so much noise at the time Rhodd didn't know Dad joined him in that dark hole. He could see Rhodd's back but didn't know how to let his friend know he was there without scaring him. Rhodd might shoot him, thinking that he was another German soldier, so he talked like a white man imitating and Indian: "Ugh, Indians heap big warriors. They make it hard on German pale-faces." Rhodd was startled to hear someone talking in the night so close to him, but he laughed so hard at the ethnic references, Dad knew he was safe.

The stories flowed at times, and so many of them remained unfinished:

- Two German soldiers came out of the forest dressed like GIs and walked into the American's chow line. They soon realized they made a mistake and tried to escape.

- Dad swam the Rhine River three times in the winter to scout the enemy even though there was no way to get warm in the cold except to drip dry.

- His unit broke through the German frontline in a surprise night attack and found prostitutes with the German soldiers in the fox holes to keep them from deserting.

- "Lah We Lah His" ("All Hell Can't Stop Us!") was on one insignia of his uniform. This Pawnee Indian saying symbolized much of his attitude towards life.

Now, the green fields of corn are laid by. The farmers prepare their machinery for fall harvest. I remember Dad working the corn harvest each year. Often, he would get only 3-4 hours of sleep at night. He had a tremendous capacity for physical work for such a small man: 5' 10" and 140 lbs. His Army field jacket was a size 34. How he carried full combat gear that exceeded 100 pounds, ran, and fought still amazes me.

Dad loved his horses and Nebraska; he never wanted to move elsewhere after the war. He was a good cowboy: contrary, stubborn, and fiercely loyal to this country.

His last meal before going to the hospital was sweet corn, mashed potatoes, gravy, steak, green beans, and black coffee. He ate more than I did. I saw him eat that same meal a thousand times, and I was raised on it, too.

Only something alive can die, and Dad lived every day. He may not have been very organized, forward looking, or reflective, but he never let a joke pass him by. His sense of place was Richardson Country.

A few years ago, Bette Davis was on *The David Letterman Show*. He asked her flippantly, "How is it, getting older?" She coolly answered, "It ain't for sissies." Living is tough, and for Dad, dying wasn't easy either. His heart was strong until the end, but both lungs were cancerous and became filled with fluid.

When I walked into his room at 9 a.m. that last day, it was a beautiful, summer, morning. His eyes looked brighter than the day before. He joked and called his granddaughter a "runt." He looked around the room to see who was there, but he faded in and out of awareness. An hour later, things started to change. He panted. His eyes rolled back a little; he became unconscious and was not awake after that.

His room, number 101, signified new lessons to learn on a different journey. His blue, feet foreshadowed the end and symbolized his body starting to shut down, one system at a time, as that color slowly marched toward his face. It climbed to his knees, then to his waist. His kidneys stopped. Muscles twitched. I could hear pneumonia fill his lungs, as he drowned from the inside. The two oxygen tanks connected to him were not enough.

I stood at the foot of his bed. He took one slow, long gulp of air, then a second, and held his breath. His face turned scarlet, and his head slowly fell to his right side. He did not breath again.

I looked out the window of his room and saw the Earth as he knew it: grass, trees, and sky. His van faced the window. The American flag flew in a strong, summer breeze. A cottonwood tree stood tall. This trinity marked my father: a van to roam (a modern cowboy), the US flag (nothing made him more proud), and the tree (Nebraska's state symbol).

Going through his military records after the funeral, I found a telegram to Mother from the US War Department saying her husband was released from the hospital and returned to active service on July 31, 1944. Fifty years later to the day, he died and was released from life. The curtain fell for the last time. He wore out, but he didn't rust out. He never quit. He fought for life, every breath, to the end. He was just a man, but he was my father.

> "The grave itself is but a covered bridge
> leading from light to light, through a brief darkness."
>
> -Henry Wadsworth Longfellow

22

My Friends Are Books

"Asked whether he liked books, Mark Twain said that
he liked a thin book because it would steady a table,
a leather volume because it would strop a razor, and
a heavy book because it could be thrown at a cat."

-Otto Bettmann

Books are addictive. I can not stay away from them. They entrap and seduce me with their knowledge and wisdom. I do not spend my money on many things, but what I have left over usually goes for books. I have seven bookcases in the house; all of them are full, and I am trying to figure out how to get a couple more. Then, I will have to decide where to put them. Libraries and bookstores are almost impossible for me to escape, because the books on the shelves appear to be saying, "Take me! Read me first!"

One thing I learned from books is I have been unable to judge them by their covers. Some of the best ones that I read looked awful on the outside. People should not be judged by their outward appearances, either. What we think we see on the cover is not necessarily what we get from the inside.

Good books are good friends. People can take them anywhere anytime. In the solitude of a quiet room or the congestion of a busy airport, a friend is as close as my book and can be there as quickly as I can turn a page.

I still believe that the eyes of my true friends light up a little when I walk into the room. Acquaintances will notice me probably, but friends acknowledge me with an intensity of fire, and a certain degree of passion will show through their eyes. Some people call the eyes "gateways to the soul," and I believe them. Many books have put that spark of intensity and concern into my eyes. The warmth, tenderness, and compassion of a growing relationship can exist between two people,

93

a pet and his master, or between a reader and his book.

Benjamin Franklin once said, "If you want to be remembered after you are gone, either do things worth writing about or write things worth reading." By reading, I can contact the greatest minds that ever walked the Earth.

Books extend the mind and are helpers in many ways. Books are magic carpets of the imagination and can take us to far off lands or help us on spiritual journeys. What makes us vulnerable also makes us strong. If books are my weakness, then they are my strength, also. Everyone has weaknesses, but not everyone turns them into strengths. What weak points could we turn into strengths with a little work?

Books are symbolic of life. They have beginnings and endings, prologues and epilogues. The chapters in between the covers show various stages of development and growth. A good book is a guide which leads us, has clarity of vision, and a curiosity about tomorrow's experiences. These new friends possess keys to doors that let us into rooms previously unknown and locked.

The knowledge found in these exciting places challenges us and adds zest to our living. With this help we search our emotions, learn about others, develop our dreams, and grow ourselves.

I find it impossible to read without taking personal inward journeys. Some are suspenseful; some are fantasies; some are wonderful discoveries that help make life worth living. When I find a stirring conflict in a "hot plot," I lose myself for a time. This escape is what meditation is meant to be: peaceful, solitary, enlightening, and enjoyable.

Do you want increased wisdom, awareness, foresight, insight, and creativity? If so, then more reading is just what you need. Commit yourself to increasing your vocabulary. Like the library association says, "Jog your mind today; run to the library." Make your whole body healthy. "Open a book, then open your mind and say, 'AHHHHHHHHHH!' "

23

Never

"Never, never, never, never give in."

-Sir Winston Churchill

Dear Ashley,

Ashley Pilar Martin
Bergan Mercy Hospital
Oakdale Elementary School
Westside Middle School
Westside High School
Kappa Alpha Theta
University of Nebraska
The World of Work
The United States of America
Distant Lands
Foreign Countries
The World
The Universe
The Mind of God

Trying to find the right mailing address and zip code to send this letter to you was a daunting task. My favorite American play is Thornton Wilder's *Our Town*. When you read it, you will understand the above address that I wrote for you here.

I know where you were in the past. I know where you are now. Where will you be in the future? I am as excited as you are to think where you might go when your college life ends.

Thinking of tomorrow is fun, but what is important is what you do with "now." Like the saying goes, "Yesterday is history. Tomorrow is a mystery. Today is a gift. That's why we call it 'the present.' " As you

95

are working on creating your future, don't forget to take advantage of every day, and enjoy the friends you meet along the way.

I remember so many good times together as you grew up. One day, I was reading the newspaper when you were almost two years old. I was not aware that you were on the other side of the table pretending to read a page of the paper yourself until I put my section down and saw you there so engrossed. The page was bigger than you were. You were quiet and serious. Your eyes were focused and intent. Only when I saw the page was upside down did I realize you were not going to read for one more year.

When you were three years old, I was typing in the den, and you watched me. I forgot about you for awhile, as I worked on my letter. All of a sudden, you said, "Daddy, you are so wealthy." In surprise, I stopped working and saw you sitting on the floor by my feet pulling paper out of the wastebasket.

When I said, "What do you mean?"

You said, "Daddy, You are rich. You have so much paper that you can throw all this away. Can I have some?"

When you were in the fourth grade, I started reading to you Robert Frost's poem, "Stopping By Woods On a Snowy Evening." It did not take more than two readings before you heard the trotting rhythm of the horse between the lines, as the man headed home through the evening's darkness and falling snow. When I asked you to read it, you eagerly did so. When I asked you to say the first line from memory, you did not think you could, but you tried. The second line came along soon after, then the third, and the fourth. In two minutes, you memorized the first verse correctly. We worked on the rest of the poem together for twenty minutes, and you completed all of it.

As we recited it together from memory for your mother, another part of your character kicked in when you said, "Let's see how fast we can say it." I tried to convince you that speed was not an issue here. The important thing was to say it with feeling and understanding; however, you thought faster was better. You memorized it so well that you could say all four verses in 30 seconds without taking a breath.

When I tried to get my high school juniors in American Literature class to memorize this poem, I thought I was going to have a revolution on my hands. Those sixteen-year-olds thought it was too much work for them to do. When I said it took my fourth grade daughter, who was nine years old, only twenty minutes, they quit complaining. I convinced them to memorize the poem, but no one in my classes ever got to the point of reciting the whole thing from memory in 30 seconds. Your accomplishment is one I am proud to mention to the world. That's my girl.

Sixth grade was a good year, too. You found you could high jump better than taller girls, because you developed your leg muscles during five years of dance class. Your timing toward the bar and your kick leaving the ground were special for someone your size. One of the boys in class said you could sail like the wind over the cross bar. You still hold records at your school for track and field.

I like the fact that you have so many interests and are not afraid to try new things. I hope you continue to explore the world and appreciate all it has to offer. I think your passion for what you feel called to do will lead you to great things. "Only passions, great passions, can elevate the soul to great things" (Dennis Diderot).

I hope you don't think I am sounding too serious here, but all the ideas I learned in school were only stair-steps to the important things that came later, i.e., finding what was in my soul and how to use that to bring satisfaction in life. Of course, I want you to learn all you can in school, but I also want you to learn what you have locked in your heart. "Your soul is not a passive or a theoretical entity that occupies a space in the vicinity of your chest cavity. It is a positive, purposeful force at the core of your being. It loves without restriction and accepts without judgment" (Gary Zukav).

You have grown so much in such a short time, and I am proud of all your accomplishments. I think back to your birthday, and I remember when you came into the world. Your eyes were wide open, as though you were ready for the show to begin. I thought then, "This child will not miss much."

When times gets tough in college and life, do not forget Winston Churchill's graduation speech during WWII. Some people call it the best graduation speech ever given. Its message consists of only six words: "Never, never, never, never give in."

What else does a college student need to know at graduation? Most difficulties can be overcome, if one does not quit. People are never beaten, until they give in. The best angle in life is the "try-angle."

I know some students leave home and for whatever reason feel they can never go home, again. No matter what you do or where you travel, no matter whom you meet or what you learn, just remember that the front door of our home will always be open when you get here.

I love you,
Dad

24

Paperboy Meets the Devil:
Jabs Him in the Nose

"Life shrinks or expands
in proportion to one's courage."

-Anais Nin

I always felt safe in my small, quiet, Nebraska hometown. It reminded me of my grandmother's Currier and Ives lithographs that reflected stoic, hard working people.

One evening, the snow fell in powerful, white flurries, part of a winter storm that pelted us off and on for two straight days and nights. A thick, ivory blanket covered the streets and sidewalks as far as my young eyes could see.

Since our neighbors were conscientious homeowners, they religiously shoveled their sidewalks each day. As the snow continued to fall, the snow banks next to the sidewalks rose higher and higher, like tithes collected on church offertory plates. I had no idea that night I would look the Devil in the face.

No cars moved on the barren streets. Next to the curbs, the streetlights made the snow seem brighter against the black void above. The kitchen lights were on in every house, as people kept warm and ate their supper.

I was proud to be a paperboy. It seemed like everyone, except me, was home, safe and protected against the storm, but I was a solitary pilgrim, determined and resolute, a young man with a mission. I threw the evening news with its rubber-banded enlightenment before the front door of each home on my route.

The white papers with black newsprint that I carried every day after school were important. My two paper bags felt heavy with the weight of the world hanging from my shoulders, as I brought current events, knowledge, and the wisdom of adults to each home. I could smell the fresh ink from the printing press, and I had a job to do.

In the seventh grade, life seemed enormous, sometimes, out of control, when I heard of this country's problems, but I struggled to make sense out of my black and white world by reading. At the end of each block, if the weather was nice, I stopped and read an article, a column, or a whole page of that day's paper.

When I returned home, I wanted to talk as intelligently as I could about the day's world events with Dad. My father was a working man. He did not read much, but he read the local newspaper every day, column by column, cover to cover. He did not miss anything.

I never saw him read a book, but without saying a word, he showed me how important reading was to him, especially the newspaper. He sat at the kitchen table, oblivious to the little, family catastrophes going on around him. His sons yelled and wrestled at his feet; our collie played like one of the kids; and Mom cooked in silence. However, Dad never ate supper, until he finished reading the last page.

I liked it when he saw a certain world event in the paper as interesting and commented on it. Then I could say, "Yes, I read that." I would always try to ask him a question about the article, often going beyond the range of my youthful knowledge.

After my conversation stopped, he would lay the paper on the kitchen table, look at his twelve-year-old son, and with a surprised expression say, "I don't know. I'll think about that."

On my paper route, it was difficult to walk in my large, black overshoes. It was all I could do to fold the newspapers and throw them accurately onto the porches in the right place, without slipping and falling down on the ice and snow.

After walking in the below-freezing weather for two hours, I threw my last paper onto the porch. Every house had its news for the day, and I felt good about that. I imagined I was assisting the veteran reporters Walter Cronkite and Daniel Schorr by educating Americans, while delivering the news.

My arms and legs were tired, and my nose seemed frozen. Resolutely, I bent my head into the wind and trudged homeward, on through the snow, with a mile or more to go. I walked like a tired horse who knew his way home by heart. My head was down to protect myself from the elements, and I did not look up.

I was always hungry. I imagined that I could smell Mom's dinner cooking in the kitchen. She would be finishing the chicken, mashed potatoes, gravy, and warm bread for supper. I knew my brothers were wrestling on the floor in front of the television, while Dad smoked his cigarette and continued reading the paper.

Suddenly, like an ugly monster out of the night, I heard a frightening sound. A loud, animal growl came through the wind and assaulted my ears. I looked up, startled. The largest, blackest, and meanest looking German Shepherd dog I ever saw in my life was snarling at me from thirty feet away. As it stood there grimacing, I noticed a large chain around its neck that hung down its side and trailed away into the snow.

I started running away from him, immediately. Both empty, paper bags flapped against my hips, as I fled in panic. My heavy overshoes were no help at all, but I ran as fast as I could. I knew I was only going to live for a few minutes more before my legs would give out, and that hairy beast would bring me down.

The barking grew louder as the dog tried to catch me from behind. Fearfully, I looked over my shoulder and saw its large teeth with saliva drooling out of its mouth.

I felt lost. Instead of eating my supper at home, I thought I could soon be a meal for this large beast.

At that instant, the dog lunged from behind me and bit the paper bag hanging over my right shoulder. As he snapped down on it, his weight caused me to whip around sharply to my right. Before I knew what happened, I was pulled around 180 degrees and came to a stop, bent over at the waist, staring right into the eyes of the Devil.

In my short time on planet Earth, I never saw anything more frightening. The ministers I listened to in church never painted a picture of Satan more fearful than that face, which was inches away from me at that moment. I smelled sulfur in the wind.

The beast's heart pounded in delight, as he anticipated bringing down his prey. Passion flooded the two, coal-black eyes lying behind its black, wet nose.

My heart erupted in fear, as my pursuer's heart throbbed, eager for an end to his chase. I knew I had only moments before I would be hurt or killed. I could not put up a fight against such an animal. It weighed more than I did. It was used to fighting. I never had to struggle in my life against anything before. I didn't even know how to begin. How could I defend myself against those fangs and claws?

The creature's eyes looked like they would devour me. They were darker than the night above. They seemed to possess my soul, and I felt I was falling into them. What could I do to stop my disappearance? Is this what it is like to die?

I can not explain what happened next. The more I stared into those cruel eyes, the more curious I became in studying them. In one moment, I felt fear, and the next moment I felt wonder. I forgot about Mom, home, and dinner. I did not sense fatigue, pain, or suffering. I thought of nothing else but that moment. Time seemed to stop.

Intently, I analyzed the dog's eyes. They were eager for a fight and extremely confident. I knew I could not run away. I had no place to turn. I had no way out. I must stay and see what happened next.

I thought it strange, but I felt relief, knowing I had no options open to me right then. Unconsciously, when I made this decision, I started to relax. I inhaled deeply. The dog, tense and waiting for the right moment to pounce on me, moved to the right, then the left, trying to find his best angle for attack.

I moved with him, slowly, always facing those ebony eyes. We were dancing, but I never gave him an unprotected opening. My breathing changed from panting, like the dog, to a more relaxed pace.

The dog sensed my change in nature. At first, it felt my panic and fear. Now, it saw I did not desire to flee. I did not back up anymore. I was intrigued by what he would do next.

The dog shifted slightly and tightened its muscles to spring at me. As it composed itself, without realizing what I was doing, I attacked first. My left hand made a fist and went straight to the dog's black, wet nose. Astonished and caught off guard, my jab made it yelp and step backward. It was not hurt, just surprised. I noticed a movement in its eyes though. A cloud of confusion passed over its pupils.

Intuitively, I knew what to do next. My right hand made a fist and went directly to that black mark below its eyes. This time the dog yelped again and took another step backward.

I struck with my left hand once more, then my right. With each jab, I took a step forward into his space, as my hands found their mark. No "round house punches" here. Each movement of my fists went straight to the dog's nose. He backed up with each jab.

I felt a new confidence. The dog's teeth were still sharp and savage, but I was not the same little boy I was a few minutes before. I learned to create more strength by standing my ground with confidence.

If I was to die, I wanted to look death in the face. If a dragon was to eat me for dinner, he would have to face me to do it. If an evil spirit was going to take me away, he would have to do it with me punching his nose as hard as I could.

I witnessed the eagerness and passion of the animal's conquest slipping away. I sensed the momentum swing to my side. I still had that black, wet nose in front of me, but the fangs did not seem so long any more. I could see his breath in the cold air, but he was not as alarming now. His chest still rocked from exertion, but his legs lost their tenseness.

I summoned what little energy I had left. As I stepped forward, my left hand jabbed his nose again, but my right hand came up underneath his chin hard. I heard his mouth snap shut.

For the first time, he lowered his eyes and turned away from me. He trotted over to the curb, looked over his shoulder, once, to see if I was following him then retreated to his yard and out of sight.

I stood in the middle of the street and watched him leave, as he headed back into the darkness. Once again, I was the only thing moving in my little circle of illumination. I turned my back on that demon and headed home.

When I opened the door, struggled up the stairs, and entered Mom's kitchen, the warmth of the stove stung my cold cheeks, and I wondered if Valhalla was like this.

Too tired to say a word, I leaned against the wall and sunk to the floor. The familiar voices comforted me. The smell of my favorite meal made me remember my hunger pains. My sweatshirt was damp from sweat and clung to my shoulders. I pulled off my red, stocking hat and wet, leather gloves. My face was flushed, and I inhaled slowly, so no one would hear my lungs gasp for air.

Finally, Mom noticed my unusual state. "What happened to you? Have you been in trouble? You never looked so tired after delivering the papers."

"I ran home to eat supper," I lied. I did not want to explain my unusual experience right then, maybe later.

I looked around the room with new eyes and saw each family member in a different light. That night's emotional battle gave me a new vision, a new way of seeing my world. I knew something momentous in the stars occurred, as I looked into that animal's eyes. The dog, the Devil, or death, what ever it was changed my attitude about life. I discovered that running away from danger would never be the right answer to the problems that occurred in life.

No one spoke to me. They went on with their lives, and I was safe with mine. Slowly, I blended back into the family; however, I kept my parka on with the hood over my head and silently sat in the corner on the floor.

I thought about crying, but I was too tired. How could I tell anyone that I was almost eaten alive? Would anyone care that I almost died? Anyway, they would not believe me, I felt.

One brother would say, "You have only been gone a couple of hours. How could all that happen in such a short time in this little town? Aren't you exaggerating?"

Another brother would want to know all about it, but he was too young to understand. He would want to find the dog and re-live everything over again.

Mom would say, "Stop talking so much, and eat your dinner before it gets cold. Remember that story a few years ago about the monster that lived under your bed upstairs?"

Dad would look at me, not say anything at all, and turn to the next page of the paper.

I chose not to make a scene and draw attention to myself. I summoned my remaining strength to unzip my coat and hang it up in the hallway.

"Thank you," I said, when Mom handed me an empty plate.

Mom was the best cook ever, and I was thankful she was there. A few minutes ago, I wasn't sure I would ever eat again. I filled my plate, sat down at the table, and watched my family in silence. For the first time in my life, I said a taciturn prayer, just for me, then, I savored every mouthful of that meal. I knew I was lucky to be alive, and I understood the meaning of "grace." I would have to grow up before I learned the word "epiphany."

It took a long time, but Dad finally commented on a story in the paper. I didn't look up and kept on eating. He stared at me, as though waiting for me to speak. I smiled and shrugged my shoulders. No story in the paper that night meant as much to me as the one I just lived through. Some day, I would tell it.

25

Running in the Dark

"Obstinacy never got a man anywhere."

-Herodotus

I know people can walk in their sleep. I acknowledge how it can happen. However, I never knew anyone, personally, who did. Certainly, I never felt that it could happen to me.

I like to make goals. I enjoy facing challenges involving personal discipline, and some people call me stubborn. One winter day, I decided to run a marathon, 26 miles and 385 yards. The race was six months away, but I was determined to do my best. Religiously, I devoted part of each day to this objective.

Without missing a day of training for four months, habitually, I rose from a deep sleep at 5:30 a.m. The music that woke me was soon unnecessary, because I learned to sense the click of the falling numbers on the digital alarm clock swinging into place seconds before that prearranged moment. My body rolled toward the side of the bed before the FM station invaded my bedroom.

My three-year-old German Shepherd accompanied me on these daily jogs and learned my course so well that he could run off-leash with no verbal commands. He led me through our early morning challenge and came to greet me with his cold, wet nose against my right shoulder before my feet touched the floor.

As a child, I conditioned myself to get out of bed and get dressed at my father's command, in my sleep if necessary, so I could do chores with him on the farm. This training let me awake in time to make it to my early classes in college after studying into the early hours of the morning. I always made it on time after cramming for an exam the night before, as I worked my way through school.

This morning was no different. I rolled to my right. Slowly, my head moved upward when the waterbed shimmered like agitated Jell-O in a plastic mold, as my body weight localized on my elbow.

Both feet swung over the side of the bed. In one motion, they fell to the floor. My upper torso rose to a vertical position poised on the mattress. My wrists, fingers, and toes propelled me unknowingly onto my feet. Disciplined by this routine from childhood, I never stopped or altered my rhythm.

One foot at a time punctured the black holes at the bottom of each leg of my sweat pants. I tied a knot in the string around my waist with my right hand, while the left hand negotiated a brightly colored sweatshirt and hood. My feet automatically wiggled into the white, cotton socks, and the blue, nylon, waffle-soled, marshmallow-cushioned, running shoes. So swift and effortless were my movements, my heart seemed still asleep.

I didn't bother to turn on any lights, because I had performed this ritual so many times before. I walked through the house in the dark. I took four steps from the bed to the door, seven more down the hall, turned right, five paces to the front door, unlocked it, and then I was outside. Effortlessly, I moved into the night. There were no lights or groans from any disturbed family members, just peace, silence, and the darkness of morning.

As I went through the door, I tilted my head forward. My body felt the pull of gravity. Down the front yard and following the pavement, I was on my way.

I jogged down the hill, coasted one block, negotiated the dirt road through the city park, snaked down the bicycle path to the baseball field, traversed the gravel parking lot, climbed up the access road to the main street, and loped down the sidewalk to the corner. I passed one landmark after another, all expected, anticipated, and familiar.

Suddenly, I was aware of the screech of tires on pavement. A loud car horn blared in my right ear. My dog yelped an unexpected warning. A round, hazy, red light appeared through my unconsciousness.

All those sounds and impressions were on the fringe of my awareness anyway, because I heard them numerous times before on my runs, but they never came all at one time.

Then both of my legs bumped into a firm, metallic object. That unusual feeling got most of my attention. I had never felt that object before on any of my runs. It wasn't supposed to be in my path. I tried to move my legs, but the object wouldn't let me go.

107

I started to get mad because I knew I had to hurry through the run to get home with enough time to shower and change, so I could get to work. It was then that I finally opened my eyes for the first time that morning.

Standing in the middle of a major intersection, leaning against the side of a 1976 Oldsmobile, I looked over the car's hood, directly into a red traffic light. My dog stared, apprehensively, at me from the safety of the sidewalk on the other side of the street.

I heard three people angrily yelling at me over the tops of their rolled down car windows.

"You joggers! You dummies! You think you own the sidewalks and the streets. We could have killed you! You don't know how lucky you are! They ought to take exercising off the streets and put it back into the bedrooms of this city where it belongs. All you jogging morons should run in bed where you won't get hurt, especially at 5:30 in the morning."

When they saw I wasn't injured and no damage had been done, they drove off in a huff, shouting unkind obscenities at me, saying something about how car drivers today aren't safe from joggers anymore, and running should only be allowed after it was daylight, not before.

Sheepishly, I turned around and walked home. I walked! I didn't run a step. My legs were shaking so badly I don't think I could have run two steps without falling down anyway. That shocking ordeal left me quivering for days, and even now, my stomach gets nauseous when I think about this harrowing experience.

I ran my marathon as planned and finished it. My body felt electrified for three days. My legs ached for a week. I reached my goal, but I never ran another race of that distance again. My ego was satisfied, at last.

I still think I am lucky to be alive after that morning run in the dark. That experience caused me to form several resolutions about life that I follow still.

Now, I do not attempt anything in the dark, literally or metaphorically. Before putting one foot in front of the other, I make sure my eyelids can stay open without assistance. I removed "5:30 a.m." from my vocabulary and added "somnambulism" to it.

Herodotus was right. I don't need to be so obstinate. Life is full of challenges. Why should I be so determined to have my own way? Not yielding to reason and acting mulish are not the best ways to succeed in life.

I am more understanding of sleepwalkers. Instead of laughing at those stories, now, I remember when I ran, not walked, a mile in my sleep before I woke up and lived to tell about it.

26

Sacrifice

"Learn the lesson that, if you are to do the work of a prophet,
what you need is not a scepter but a hoe."

-Bernard of Clairvaux

The word sacrifice usually makes me sweat. Giving myself to
something larger and blending into the "good" life often equals hard
work, perspiration, and surrendering things of value. When times are
tough, I don't see many people choosing to pick up their hoes in place of
their swords.

Unless my friends follow religious traditions like Christmas,
where it is better to give than to receive, or Lent, which has forty days of
fasting and penitence, or tithing, where 10% of one's income is given to
the church, it seems that most people only think of themselves. The "Me
Generation" still lives.

Casey Camp Horinek, one of my friends, is an exception. She
is a Native American medicine woman from the Ponca Tribe. For years,
she was the only woman who attended Crow Dog's Paradise on the
Rosebud Sioux Reservation in South Dakota. In August of each year, she
participated in the annual Sun Dance ceremonies.

Sun Dances are holy affairs for Native Americans on the plains.
Usually, only men participate because it is a rugged affair that includes
fasting, endurance, hours of dancing, praying, pain, and sacrifice.

Then there is the piercing. Many times, I have seen the scars on
the male Indians' chests. These wounds, voluntarily accepted, prove to
the tribe that the dancers have the determination needed to accept the
commands of the Great Spirit. Leather tongs are attached at one end
to a cottonwood tree. The other end is slipped under the dancers' skin,
males to the chest-females to the back, and tied in knots, symbolically
attaching them to the "Tree of Life." The dancers move in the sun, sing,
and pray. Later, when they fall to the ground exhausted and unconscious,

the leather straps rip from their bodies, tearing the skin. These two inch scars are later worn with sacred pride, like badges of honor.

Casey is a quiet woman with fire in her eyes. She talks softly, and every word counts. There is a measured pace to each sentence that reaches just so far. Then another sentence falls softly in front of her, as though she stalks game through a forest of thoughts, stepping around metaphorical thorn bushes, missing sharp rocks, wading through streams, and stopping to enjoy the beauty of a meadow. Look for her in the movie version of *Black Elk Speaks*.

Casey is a wise woman. Wherever she goes, children surround her. They constantly wait on her and eagerly enjoy doing so. Her black hair is long, below her waist. It has never been cut. For each family meal, she places small portions of each course on a plate, and away from the crowd, she offers them to the six grandfathers.

I smoked a peace pipe with her once in a group of twenty, after she returned from a Sun Dance. The experience was emotional. The tobacco was a mixture of Red Willow bark, sage, sweet grass, and tobacco. We thought of personal prayers we wanted answered and symbolically sent them aloft with the ceremonial pipe smoke.

The sweat lodge ceremony she led after that was a sacrifice and caused me to really sweat. Twenty people sat shoulder to shoulder in a five foot high by twelve foot across, circular lodge. This experience was a compressed community experience. An enormous fire heated rocks for eight hours, and they were placed in a pit in the center of our circle to provide an instant sauna. For two hours, the rocks kept coming, and the air in the lodge got hotter and hotter. At one point, I thought my hair was on fire.

Casey was peaceful and calm, wearing a full length robe in that 140 degree heat. I have never been so hot in my life. We meditated in complete blackness and sweat. I couldn't see my hands in front of my face, but the heat pushed me back against the wall and down to the ground. I felt like a 2,000 pound buffalo was sitting on my chest. If I had any anger or hostility in me then, it was melted away in that Native American temple.

After our group finished praying and I pulled back the flap, I saw the stars in the sky and smelled the cool night air. I understood the symbolism of the lodge and felt how good it was to work for something larger than myself. I sacrificed my time, convenience, and comfort to learn to see with the eyes of a different culture than my own.

Standing in the night next to the lodge, ideas raced through my mind. I felt rejuvenated and the inevitability of death confronting me in the second half of my life. I must stop looking for easy answers in my remaining days. I felt in my bones the meaning of sacrifice. I must offer my time to an altar symbolizing something larger than myself. The question of importance was, "To what altar do I sacrifice my remaining days?"

Carl Jung, the Swiss psychiatrist, sacrificed what he thought was his complete medical career when he split with Sigmund Freud in the early 1900s. Freud wanted Jung to promote his idea that sex and the parental relationships of the patient were the primary forces behind individual psychological problems. Jung was confident that "the sacrifice of the ego" was most important and the aim of true individuation.

James Hillman felt the meaning of sacrifice was to return human events to God, "For sacrifice, as we all know and always forget, means connecting personal human events with their impersonal divine background." Killing old dogmas are the sacrifices we make to live our lives in new, positive ways.

What would happen if we always lived our lives with honesty, wrote letters that told the truth, and acted like our lives might end any minute, any hour, and any day? People would play fewer games. There would be fewer lies. Letters would be shorter. Fewer words would be spoken, but they would mean much more. There would be more action by people knowing they didn't have forever.

The sacrifices required to write books are great. Many texts were written in jails, because the authors were difficult for societies to tame. Jail was a safe place to put troublemakers. The forced solitude in jail became the power of the genie. The writers consolidated their dissatisfaction with life and used this time to record their thoughts in coherent form. The flames started by these authors, as they rubbed their pages together, created fires of hatred and enlightenment that often changed world history.

The following works came from prisons around the world: Thomas Malory-*Morte de Arthur*, Adolf Hitler-*Mein Kampf*, Mohandas Gandhi-*Autobiography*, Martin Luther King, Jr.,-"Letters from a Birmingham Jail," Karl Marx-*The Communist Manifesto*, John Bunyan-*Pilgrim's Progress*, and Miguel de Cervantes-*Don Quixote*. While reading these books, we learn every achievement was once considered impossible. If there were no problems, there would be no opportunities.

The simple things are the most satisfying. There is no elevator to success. We have to take the stairs. We grow only when we push ourselves beyond what we already know. Never underestimate the potential and power of the human spirit. Everyone has something to teach. Like the power of the genie which comes from being trapped in such a small space for so long, the power of sacrifice often produces an epiphany, a warm and blissful revelation of truth.

27

Seven Good Men

"If a man has done his best, what else is there?"

-General George S. Patton

Seven men were very close to me. My association with them made me feel many emotions: respect, contempt, happiness, sorrow, love, and anger. They taught me a lot about living a happy life, and I pray I never forget them.

****

George, a minister, was thirty-five years old, although he looked much older. No longer could he support his religion and church. Day after day, he forced himself to work at tasks, which did not involve his heart's passion. The only thing that kept him in the ministry was the feeling he would let God down and be a disgrace to his family if he left. After suffering a massive heart attack caused by this stress, he became paralyzed with severe speech impediments. He became unemployed, lived on workman's compensation insurance, and felt unsure in his own mind if he could ever hold another job. He under went weekly psychiatric therapy, because he felt angry. He was bitter about the trick God and fate played on him. George's wife could not stand his self-torture. She wanted out; she could not live happily, seeing her husband in doubt, unfulfilled, confused, and aimless. She moved out of their home and sought a divorce. In deep depression, George slashed his wrists with a razor blade and swallowed a bottle of sleeping pills. His suicide attempt matched his lifestyle for consistency. He failed at this, too.

Should he have pushed aside his guilt? Would he have been better off to follow his own conscience? In life, black and white answers seemed increasingly hard to find.

114

****

Gene was forty-five and a district sales manager for one of the largest corporations in the country. He spent twenty years in a job that he did not like, hoping to live up to his wife's expectations and support her in the style in which she was accustomed. He spent more time getting his sales staff to like him than doing a competent job with the work he was given. As a result, he developed an unacceptable, unhealthy living situation. A graduate engineer, he always wanted to work with machines rather than customers, distributors, and sales promotions. It was obvious he did not like his work. Two months after I last saw him, he suffered a massive heart attack which kept him from doing any more of that unpleasant business.

Is it possible a heart attack was the only acceptable way for him to get out of that difficult position? Now, he can save face and still live the life he wants.

****

Roy, a thirty-nine-year-old sales representative with two children, fell to the dirty, asphalt parking lot of an Omaha grocery store on a hot, dusty, August afternoon. The store was his most frustrating and obnoxious account. Just before leaving this last call of the day, he talked to another sales representative about the many unpleasant things filling up his life at the time. He did not like his job, but it paid well, and his family depended on him. He could not let them down.

When a passing shopper saw him lying next to his car and attempted mouth- to-mouth resuscitation, his face turned blue. The rescue squad arrived quickly, but his heart stopped beating. He was pronounced dead on arrival at the closest hospital. If Roy lived his life with a different attitude, would his life have been lengthened?

****

Carl was a calm, quiet, unassuming person on the outside. Raised in the Italian section of South Omaha, he learned early in life how to work hard, take care of himself, and get revenge on his enemies. He took pride in doing his job correctly, the same way, for thirty years.

115

When he was not working as a purchasing agent, he acted and looked like someone's old, sad grandfather, but if people tried to cheat, lie, and steal from him once, they never stood on his good side again.

Four years ago, he could have retired at sixty-two. He chose not to do so, because he wanted revenge from his boss who cheated him out of a raise and to punish a younger man who was groomed to replace him when he left. He tried to make it as hard for these two people as he could. Three years of hate, vengeance, and backbiting ended last year when Carl died of a heart attack, one month before he finally agreed to retire, to leave his boss alone, and to give up his job to the younger man.

This all-consuming hostility permeated every aspect of his personal life and leisure time. His wife talked about his negative attitude. His son talked about his anger with friends and relatives. Carl talked about his unhappiness at the racetrack, at football games, and on vacations. His power within the business association was so strong that the other members in the group would not allow the general manager to fire him. The bulk of each day for over three years was spent tormenting these two people, who he felt, looked down on his abilities. Revenge was his only remaining passion.

Did hatred make Carl happier? I doubt it, and I am sure it shortened his life.

****

Larry was thirty-four years old and the father of two children. He owned two department stores and everything a man could want materially. He worked hard to get what he had at such an early age, a great deal for one so young. When he bought a new home, Larry was overweight but active in certain sports and community activities. Before his family finished unpacking the last box that the movers brought, he collapsed on the court, while playing handball at a local recreational center. Despite expert assistance from the staff and quick ambulance transportation to the nearest hospital, he died.

How much material reward in this life is enough to make us happy?

****

I went to college with Jack and his wife in Lincoln. He was a humorous, calm person. He wanted life to always be a good time, but he was overly conscientious toward his duties, responsibilities, and work. Just mention politics, and he would talk for days without catching his breath. Recently, I received my monthly issue of the Nebraska Alumnus Magazine and noticed in the obituary column, "Jack_____, 34, dead Washington, D.C., class 1967."

After a phone call, I learned that an unexpected heart attack toppled Jack to the floor, after a long, exhausting day at work.

****

Everybody who knew him thought Mike was a happy man, because he always spoke pleasantly to everyone he met. He was involved in many community projects, with a rented house, married, and two children who called him "Dad." His insurance agency grew steadily, and he was considered for a management promotion with his company. Every free minute of his leisure time was spent hunting and fishing. Many people thought these sports were his job. They imagined selling insurance was only something to fill in periods of time when his golf slice was a particular problem, the duck season was over, or the fish were not biting in the county, anywhere.

Few people knew that he did not like the town where he lived, and he found it hard to find friends his age with similar interests. He felt pressured to buy a lot, build a house, pay off his child's unusually large doctor bills, buy a new car, take a vacation, please his parents, and live up to the expectations of his in-laws. Few knew about his feelings when he did not finish college, or his youngest brother graduated from a large university with honors and got a prestigious job with a big company in the East. Mike often talked to me about how he would prefer to be a game warden or work for a conservation agency.

At thirty-one, Mike suffered a massive heart attack at home in front of his wife and two children, who were six and three years old, respectively. His agonizing death at such a young age was a shock to us all. The attack started and ended in ten minutes. Could he have lived longer by living his life his way?

****

In the last twelve months, these seven, close friends suffered heart attacks. One is still alive. Can I afford not to understand what their lives mean to me? Many men are in agony, because they accept a slave-like approach to life. Many males see jobs, parents, wives, children, and bosses as excuses for not doing with their lives what they want. Responsibilities, duties, guilt trips, "oughts" and "shoulds" straight-jacket too many males into becoming obedient servants of others instead of learning to take care of themselves.

How long can I look and not see what is happening around me? Too many men are walking to the gallows before their time. They may be smiling. Expensive possessions may surround them. Retirement plans might bulge with unspent money. Their children might have orthodontically correct braces. They might have an extra car in the garage, and their wives may have a gorgeous fur coat hanging in the closet.

So what? These men will continue to die before their time or be incapacitated. Too often, I notice that hollow laugh of affected pomposity, which comes from men obsessed by their own self-importance. Their minds fill with notions of grandeur, power, and greed. Their messages are deafening.

I still can see these seven friends of mine everyday in my memory. I pray that I learn from them, so I can use every hour of my life in positive and productive ways. I do not want to waste a moment of this gift called "life." Filling my days with non-essential tasks is not the answer to happiness.

28

John Steinbeck:
A Twentieth Century Transcendentalist

"This I believe: That the free, exploring mind of the individual human
is the most valuable thing in the world. And this I would fight for:
the freedom of the mind to take any direction it wishes, undirected.
And this I must fight against: any idea, religion, or government
which limits or destroys the individual."

-John Steinbeck

To be "transcendental" is to rise above, to surmount, to go
beyond, to climb over the mountain top or scale the heights of a barrier.
Immanuel Kant gave the name "transcendentalism" to this philosophy as
it originated in Europe, but the definition changed, substantially, when
it came to the United States in the nineteenth century. In this country,
people use the term to seek the supernatural everywhere, a glory of
complete perfection, to be independent of the Deity in relation to the
universe. Spirit transcends matter, and we learn to see Nature and Beauty
in the abstract, as we rise to a general and transcendent truth.

I have always been drawn to these ideas. Many people, when
thinking of transcendentalism, refer to Ralph Waldo Emerson and Henry
David Thoreau, famous nineteenth century Unitarian ministers and
philosophers. John Steinbeck did much to encompass the ideas of these
gentlemen and presented them in a contemporary twentieth century
package.

Since I was in junior high school, I dreamed of reading all the
works of a major writer, the good and the bad, so I could understand his
or her development as an artist and a person, from the pre-success stage
to the post-success stage, to observe the writer's personality changes
during this process, to notice what ideas the author hung his literary
reputation on and why those particular ones were chosen. I wanted to

feel, as much as possible, what it was like to experience that light of originality and birth of inspiration, which preceded a literary classic.

Over the last several years, I read every book, play, and short story John Steinbeck published during his life, those published by his family, posthumously, and many written about him. He produced seventeen books of fiction, plus other movie scripts, plays, newspaper articles and short stories. I read over thirty books by and about this man. I value the stories' messages, and I find him a delightfully warm and compassionate man.

I fully expected to find another "Hemingway" when I started this quest. At the beginning of my literary search, I did not want to find another egocentric, macho character that should have been in his books rather than writing them, like "Papa" was. In Steinbeck, I found a male writer filled with human understanding, a flexible author whose characters are believable and carry personal messages that speak to me.

Steinbeck was "cussed" and discussed during the four decades he wrote fiction. Many critics never recognized he won a Noble Prize for Literature, was nine times on the best seller lists with eight different titles over a period of twenty-five years. This feat has never been duplicated by any other American author.

He wrote eight hours a day, six days a week, for forty years. He would sharpen twenty-four pencils each morning and write with them until each one was blunt. After many years of this regimen, he had to use his left hand to insert a pencil into the calluses on his writing hand, because he was unable to pick it up with his right hand. Every few months, he would sandpaper those calluses, so he could continue to write. It is hard for me to ignore this man because of my respect for the human being behind his books, but the messages in his writing are what I really want to discuss.

Known as "the California giant," Steinbeck said: "If nature failed, so did the people. Life on the land is divided by the movement of rains and success or failure of the harvest. When the soil loses its water, individuals and families crack and dry up. The promises of their lives harden into silence and hungry despair."

Steinbeck felt in all of his work there was a primary, ageless question confronting the history of mankind, the relationship of people to nature. Tied to his feelings regarding transcendentalism and the land, subordinate to them, in fact, are his ideas about "is" thinking and "non-teleological" thought. "Is" thinking becomes the concern primarily not with what should be, or could be, or might be, but rather with what actually necessitates a natural look at life, objective evaluation, and women who feel they can shape their own destinies. "Is" thinking brings us to a new level of gentleness and a desire to reach out and hug our fellow human beings in warmth, acceptance, and compassion.

Teleological thinking is to always know the cause and effect of things. Non-teleological thinking is to realize that we are small beings, not at the center of the universe, and we only have one point of view of how things in nature are running. He said: " . . . people looking at reality bring their own limitations to the world. If they have strength and energy of mind, the tide pool stretches both ways, digs back to electrons and leaps space into the universe and fights out of the moment into non-conceptual time. Then ecology has a synonym which is all."

Non-teleology is looking at a mountain and realizing the summit may or may not be as far as we can see. If a climber goes as far as possible, he might be limited by training, supplies, stamina, and weather. Factors controlled and uncontrollable will determine the distance one can travel. When the climber reaches what may appear to be the top because the incline stops, that does not mean the climb is over. The climber's vision may be obscured, and clouds may cover the next incline.

Of the six hundred characters that appear in Steinbeck's books, Jim Casy appeals to me most. In my opinion, the lonely preacher personified most of what Steinbeck tried to suggest to the reader about how to live a proper life, respect others, be a good citizen, and think religiously. To summarize all Casy implied, we should remember his line in *The Grapes of Wrath*: "All that lives is holy!"

Casy was a preacher but left the calling, because he questioned his personal motives and was confused about his own directions in life. Casy decides: "I ain't gonna preach . . . I ain't gonna baptize. I'm gonna work in the green fields, and I'm gonna be near to folks. I ain't gonna try to teach 'em nothing. I am going to try to learn . . . Oh, I am a talker . . . No getting away from that. But I am not preaching. Preaching is telling folks stuff. I am asking them. That ain't preachin', is it?"

The Grapes of Wrath is a perfect example of Steinbeck's own realistic awareness of the need for personal action. He worked in the fields with the migrants. He became known as "Migrant John." Once, he went nearly four days without sleep and gave all his own clothes, blankets, money, and food to the starving children and workers he met along the way, the ones too weak or helpless to help themselves. When he returned home, he burned a 60,000 word manuscript of the book he was currently writing, a humorous account of the migrants in southern California, and plunged non-stop into *The Grapes of Wrath*.

Steinbeck was forever changed when he saw a dead child carried out of a "Hooverville Camp," because she was so anemic she could not get out of her cot by herself when the flood waters rose and drowned. This scene in real life compelled the sympathetic Steinbeck to write compulsively for nine months until the bestselling book was finished. After he mailed the manuscript to his publisher, he checked into the local hospital with a nervous breakdown.

For Steinbeck, work was an outward expression of prayer. Call it active meditation; call it blue-collar Karma. Through his characters, Steinbeck united the gospel of work with man's need for spiritual and intellectual fulfillment.

"The last clear definite function of man, muscles aching to work, minds aching to create beyond the single need, this is mankind. For (people) unlike any other thing, organic or inorganic, in the universe grows beyond his work, walks up the stairs of his concepts, emerges ahead of his accomplishments."

A transcendentalist, Steinbeck was not interested in politics, although he was a loyal Johnson Democrat. His politics were of the heart. Steinbeck asserted his belief in all people having the ability to find their own place with dignity in this life, to find their own gods in order to handle their own personal needs. His characters tried to be part of a larger group, but first they established their own individualism. All his characters were on their way to becoming part of the living whole that is life.

For him, respectability was a dead end and supported the accepted cultural value system that presumed final answers. Many of his characters are failures in society but are living successes, because they choose to avoid society's problems that cause society to fail. To live only for respectability is no longer respectable.

Steinbeck shares ideas that some would find to be like Spinoza, where all things are interrelated. Man becomes just another cog in the machinery of life. Much of our American way of life is non-essential, harmful to others and nature, and slowly we are killing ourselves because of it. This is why the land owners in California placed a price on the author's head after *The Grapes of Wrath* was published. A hit man was arrested, and charges were filed against the initiator of this failed plot.

Steinbeck, like Emerson, Whitman, and Thoreau would have done, condemned the man-centered attitude toward the environment fostered by the Judeo-Christian ethic in which everything in nature exists solely to serve mankind. Instead, with his fiction, Steinbeck created a pastoral economy that is suited to mankind and nature that protects both. A retreat to the simple life is what he proclaimed. Vociferously, he stated the main problems we face today in our world stem from the self-serving attitudes of men and women.

When Steinbeck discovered, at the age of four, that "high" rhymed with "fly," he started composing poetry. He read *Le Morte De'Arthur* at the age of six and *Beowulf* at eight. He existed on twenty-five dollars a month for food when he began writing. He said he and his first wife survived on "mountains of beans." He was a person who always knew what he wanted to do in life, write. He tore up two novels before he decided to sell a third. He wrote four more before one was sold. He threw away another novel after finishing five, and one of his dogs destroyed a nearly completed manuscript.

The third novel, *To a God Unknown,* was the one before *Tortilla Flat,* his first book to make any money. I always liked the title *To a God Unknown,* because it represents my feelings about the life force controlling us all, a sense that something is above all of us, that a power greater than humanity is there for all of us to discover in our own way.

A line Steinbeck used in the poem in the foreword of this book comes from the *Vedas.* "Who is He to whom we shall offer our sacrifice?" *Veda* means knowledge or sacred lore. *The Vedas* are a collection of over one hundred books in Sanskrit and are the sacred writings of the Hindus. This question is a universal one, and Paul addresses the same question in Acts 17:22-29.

Steinbeck confronted this issue in his acceptance speech for the Nobel Prize in Stockholm in 1962. He said: "We have usurped many of the powers we once ascribed to God. Fearful and unprepared, we have assumed Lordship over the life and death of the whole world, of all living things. The danger and the glory and the choice rest finally in man. The test of his perfectibility is at hand. Having taken God-like power, we must seek in ourselves for the responsibility and the wisdom we once prayed some deity might have. We have become our greatest hazard and our only hope. So that today, Saint John the Apostle may well be paraphrased: In the end is the Word, and the Word is Man, and word is with Man."

29

Thankful for This Day

"Be thankful for what you have;
you'll end up having more.
If you concentrate on what you don't have,
you will never, ever have enough."

-Oprah Winfrey

In this country, most of us will have more than enough to eat. My family and friends encourage and support me in times of stress. My work satisfies me. For these and many other reasons, I am thankful. As I consider the beginning of this year, the New Year's resolution I place at the top of my list is, "I resolve to be grateful each day for all my blessings."

Many of our holidays have evolved into periods of great excesses, and the original meanings erode quickly. I hear few students and adults say they are thankful for anything, except during the month of November. The rest of the year is devoted to acquiring material possessions as fast as humanly possible.

The feast day of Thanksgiving has intrigued me since I was a child and could smell the aroma of our family's "great meal." The first famous Thanksgiving festival in 1621 was a much different occasion than our traditional one on the last Thursday of November. It was a three-day celebration held sometime between September 21 and November 9.

The fare included cod, sea bass, geese, ducks, swans, turkey, corn meal, and five deer the invited Indians brought with them. Beverages included beer, even for the kids, and water. Milk was not consumed whole at this time, and only occasionally as whey. No cider was available because apples, pears, and fruit that we take for granted now were not native to New England and would take several years to bear after transporting and planting them into the new soil. Potatoes also were not available, and neither was corn on the cob. Coffee, tea, and others foods were not known by the Pilgrims then.

Only the more important men were able to sit at the outdoor, cloth-covered tables. There were no forks on the table, only knives and a few spoons. Hands were the important utensils. They used the "reach and eat" style of dining. There were approximately 140 people at that first Thanksgiving, 90 Indian men, and 50 Pilgrims. Only four adult housewives survived that first winter, and they oversaw the cooking and preparation with children and servants helping.

It was symbolic that the Indians were at that first Thanksgiving. If it had not been for them in those early years, the new settlers would have all died from starvation and sickness.

When the Mayflower landed at Plymouth Rock, those onboard were half dead from starvation. The Indians gave them food and shelter. It was the Indians who taught the colonists how to hunt and prepare food in this new Zion. The Indians gave them corn, pumpkins, squash, beans, tobacco, peanuts, tapioca, buckwheat, melons, sugar cane, maple syrup, cranberries, and turkey.

The Indians asked for nothing in return. The sad part is this initial generosity led to their lands being stolen; they became known as savages; and they are still fighting to preserve what little is left of their home today.

A part of the 1639 document called the "Pilgrim's Resolution" justifying the white seizure of Indian lands reads, "The Earth is the Lord's and the fullness thereof, and the Earth is given to the saints, and we are the saints."

The history of this time period is fascinating. Most of us remember that the Pilgrims landed initially in 1620, and in that first year, their colony of one hundred was reduced in half to fifty people. In 1628, the Puritans began their migration with settlements in Salem and Boston, so by 1640, the Massachusetts Bay Colony grew to over 25,000 inhabitants. The Pilgrims and the Puritans wanted to purify the Church of England, the Pilgrims by separating from it and the Puritans by changing it from within. In reality, the Puritans separated from the Anglican Church by creating their own charter in the New World and not using any of the traditional English worship in their new church.

These people were filled with irony, because they did not believe in freedom of religion. They wanted to practice their religion and only their religion, so they drove others away, people like Anne Hutchinson and Roger Williams. The later ideas in this nation of separation of church and state and the Bill of Rights which guarantees freedom of speech, press, and religion would have found opponents in these early settlers.

Many Puritans would have been horrified if they knew that their early, fundamentalist churches in two hundred years would turn into more liberal churches. Of course, our secular society would totally shock them today, because the government they wanted was a theocracy, not a pluralistic republic.

Aren't there two lessons to learn in the true story of Thanksgiving? The first one must be that everyone, young and old, has multiple reasons for being thankful. All of us are dependent on the efforts of many others, past and present, for our safe and independent nation. We did not create our lives or our world, and we only partially control it, but even then, we must be thankful. The unintended good of life, as well as the intended bounty and the diversity of human culture, often works for the benefit of us all.

"However, we are involved in human destiny, a destiny which can be greater and more successful than our conceptions of it. We live a life that is not entirely ours, but our children's and our great-great-grandchildren's. This indeterminacy of history ought to make us a little more open to diversity, a little more willing to bear difficulties amid the complex forces and ambiguities of our time. In view of the twists of history, we should be a little more willing to see that even those with whom we disagree may be building the future in ways that we do not understand. While being faithful to what we think is true and right, we must be open to new possibilities for good as they emerge" (*Unitarian Universalist World Magazine*, 10/15/86).

It seems an old Viking was talking to one of the young warriors about the terrible fighting going on at the time. The young fighter was concerned about his safety. The veteran said to the young man, "There is no need to worry. What doesn't kill you outright will only serve to make you stronger."

I did not die outright from my experiences last year, and I do feel stronger. Each day is a blessing to be alive, and I am grateful.

30

The Measure of Life

"There are two worlds,
the world we can measure with line and rule,
and the world that we feel with our hearts and imagination."

-Leigh Hunt

Twelve months ago, a friend asked me, "How should I measure my life?" More than a year later, I am still wondering about my answer to that question.

Good questions have multiple levels of meaning. Like most icebergs, 90% of them are initially unseen. An answer that remains above the waterline usually misses the bulk of the question. Ask a shallow question; get a shallow answer. I try to answer a question of depth with a meaningful answer that reaches below the surface.

When I measure something, I use a standard: a ruler, calendar, scale, and odometer. To measure life, would I focus on physical things or emotional ones? Do I measure life in days and years? Do I count times of happiness, joy, pain, and sadness? T. S. Eliot's "J. Alfred Prufrock" measured life with "coffee spoons."

Writers measure life in documents, articles, and books. John Steinbeck started each day with twenty-four sharpened pencils and wrote until they were blunt. He wrote eight hours a day, six days a week, for forty years. That is how he measured his working life. Often, his writing hand possessed calluses on his fingertips so large that he couldn't pick up his pencils lying on the table. He would take a sharp knife in his non-writing hand and scrape off the dead skin, so he could write more the next day.

My grandfather, Edgar Schock, died nearly fifty years ago, and I still remember what the minister said at his funeral. In a packed church, he reminded us why so many people were there that day. We all liked my grandfather a lot. He was a humble, hardworking, simple man. He cared about people, and we cared about him.

The minister visited my favorite relative in the hospital the week before grandfather died and asked him to measure his life. The minister wanted him to reflect on what he would miss by not living on this Earth. My grandfather knew he was dying, and he was not afraid of doing so. He knew there were only a few days left for him, and he seemed to enjoy this challenge of evaluating his life.

As the minister told us this story about my grandfather, I understood why he was the most positive, male, role model for me, as I grew from a young boy into a man. He helped me decide more than any other relative what kind of person I hoped to become and how to measure my life. I remember the minister's words as though he said them yesterday.

"I will miss the simple things of life: home, family, and our farm. I will miss eating corn on the cob, listening to the St. Louis Cardinals play baseball on the radio, smelling hot-buttered popcorn, and playing cards with my friends."

The city-boy minister acted surprised. "What about the farm will you miss? All the heat and the dawn to dusk hard work?"

As he lay in his hospital bed, this wise, old man smiled at the young man who didn't understand. Their measurements of life were much different.

"No, I will miss talking to my work horses, the ones I couldn't part with when I bought my first tractor, the ones I kept for years after they were replaced. They worked for me so many years in the fields. We grew old together on the farm. I cried for days when I eventually had to sell them. I couldn't stand to see them loaded on the truck and hauled away to a sale barn. When the time finally came for the truck to leave with them, I walked away from everyone else, so no one would see me cry. They were my best friends.

Another thing I will miss will be walking down the rows of field corn in late July. The stalks then are taller than I am. The leaves are dark green.

In the evening after supper, I use to go alone to the fields and listen to the crop talk to me. I would walk deeply into the field, out of sight of the house and anyone else who might be around. The long, green leaves would rub over my shoulders and back. I loved doing that. I could smell the rich, fertile soil. I felt the coolness of the evening about to come as the sun set. I sensed a feeling of satisfaction, peace, and love like no other time of the day.

I don't know why I felt all that. I guess I just loved the land and farming as a lifestyle. Those stalks of corn caressed me as I walked, like my family was hugging me. Maybe, it was the beauty I saw in the work that I did every day. I believed all my hard work was meaningful and productive.

The farmer is an artist of the soil. I created something out of nothing. I used the horses, then the tractor, gas, seeds, soil, rain, my sweat, and imagination to paint my canvas of the land. I made a work of art in those fields each year. I felt happy and proud of what I dreamed and accomplished.

I was called to do this work. God was in those fields with me, in the dirt under my nails, in the wind lifting the pheasants above the tall grass next to the timber by the creek, and in my daughter's smile when she brought me lunch at noon. When I was in the fields, I saw beauty all around me, in the crop's potential, and the lives they would help feed.

When I was a student in 1908 at the University of Nebraska at Lincoln and pole vaulting for the track team, I developed tuberculosis, and the doctor told me to quit college and go home to recuperate. He suggested I get out of stuffy classrooms and find a physical job outdoors where I could exercise my lungs every day and breathe clean air.

Over time, he thought physical labor would restore my lungs and let me lead a long, healthy life. He also said not to overdo any physical work, because that would strain my lungs and cause a relapse. I needed steady, hard work to regain my health, but too much could kill me. That was the best medical advice I ever received. I became a farmer as a result."

As a young boy, I seldom saw my grandfather sweat. He worked hard, but he measured his tasks carefully, so he never overexerted himself. His days were calculated and productive. He never got excited. He never yelled. He got his work done. He measured everything he did in terms of energy expended. He was dependable and steady. No task was too small or too big. He handled each job in his own way and seldom asked for help.

I never saw him get angry at anyone or anything, except when he was sick and at the end of his life. Then, he was frustrated that he couldn't take care of himself anymore, and he was not self-reliant like he tried to be throughout his life.

He was quite a man, and I loved him. I still imagine him walking from the farmhouse into the cornfield before sundown to talk with God and take pride in what he accomplished on the farm that day. He was a man of few words. He said what he meant, and he meant what he said.

31

True Art at the Joslyn Museum

"Art is a collaboration between God and the artist,
and the less the artist does the better."

-Andre Gide

Recently, I took my students through the Joslyn Art Museum in Omaha. This building always gives me a feeling of peace and wisdom. Its framework captures the imagination of human nature: the uniqueness, the beauty, and the power.

I thought of George Joslyn, who started his financial empire by working for $1.25 a day unloading paper from freight cars in Des Moines, Iowa. Then, he delivered messages on his bicycle for Western Union. Later, he organized a group of boys to do the same. Within ten years, he moved from his first job to president of one of the largest corporate interests in the Midwest.

Mr. Joslyn's life was artistically framed by his business ventures, and upon his death, his wife's generosity ($3.2 million in the early 1930s) made an enormous impact on the people of Nebraska by expanding their artistic perception of the world with the museum's construction. It took 250 railroad cars to bring the pink, Georgia marble to Omaha for this monument which has become a city landmark. It corralled the finest frontier art and made an outpost of culture for this prairie state.

The artwork makes me ponder my own lifetime canvas. Making order out of chaos is designing pattern from confusion, e.g., music, painting, or writing. Whatever the medium, the composition process creates a personal genesis. We carry our own picture frames. We imagine our own canvas and how we order our lives.

What an exciting opportunity! I would rather paint my life than have someone paint it for me. Tragically, few of us know where our brushes are. This museum gives me inspiration to push back the personal barriers of my life and paint more of my individual canvas.

As I wondered how to develop my canvas, I saw my students' eyes sparkle and give away their pleasure at viewing my museum favorites. Their intense silence showed their respect for what they observed. The art of Greece, Tenochtitlan, and Timbuktu pulled my students closer to the realization that art represents life, and it is sometimes hard to know where reality ends and art begins.

We saw a vase 3,500 years old. One of the students asked, "I wonder if the ancients were very different from us?" Another said, "I feel like that vase could talk, if we just knew how to listen."

The paintings and photographs were surrounded by smooth, oak fences. The man-made boundaries shaped, molded, and limited the artistic expression of the artists. The designs were imprisoned by those clear cut and precise frames.

Some of the paintings were alive and angry about being cooped-up. They wanted to jump off the wall. I expected a couple of them to start talking to me, as I passed them. One beautiful canvas acted like it would touch me by the hand and say, "We would be good for each other. Don't you think so?"

About that time, the security guard in the room announced the museum would close in five minutes, and I realized our two hour visit was over. The guard was polite, but impatient. I suppose he had a family to go home to, deadlines to keep, and miles to go before he slept.

My students continued intently to analyze this world of imagination. They stood around me in wonder. No one made a move toward the door. In the last gallery, the students became rare paintings, masterpieces of their own. I saw some of the artistic masters that day: Rembrandt, El Greco, Titan, Bierstadt, and Catlin; but the real masterpieces, my human treasures, were Kim, Mike, John, Leslie, Noretta, Sharon, Harry, and Tiffany.

Infinity is not ringed by the same restraint as the finite world of art. Is birth and death our personal life-frame? Do we paint our own canvases with our daily lives? Will our images be happy or sad? Will we be gentle or violent? Will we be remembered or forgotten when our painting stops? Will anyone care what we produced?

Art encourages me to dream. This day, I dreamed I walked past a large, dark gallery room and noticed one spotlight suspended from the ceiling. It made a one foot, white circle on a small canvas lying on the floor. Immediately, I felt a need to paint in that lighted area. I noticed brushes and paint on a table in the corner and began to fill up the canvas with images. When I reached the frame, the surrounding darkness, I felt disappointment because I knew I must stop. I prepared to depart, but while walking away an idea came to me.

I quickly carried a chair over to the spotlight. By standing on the chair, I was just able to touch it enough to alter its beam. I moved its track lighting, so there was a little more canvas to paint. I painted it and then moved the light to paint some more, again, and again.

When morning came, I had finished painting a canvas that covered the large floor from wall to wall. Although I painted only one foot at a time, I stretched as far as I could; then I moved the light and worked some more. I pushed the frame of darkness to see a little more of my personal canvas that needed painting. So my life goes, one foot and one day at a time.

In what ways, do we see our lives as framed? Are they quiet closets where we catch our breaths away from the noisy, exhausting world? Do we envision our lives as nurturing centers for growth, where our spirits expand and take in other places and frames of mind preparing us for other times, other realities which are improvements above and beyond our present positions?

Are we content to be static, beguiled by the contemporary, or framed by dark thoughts and actions?

Can I look into the canvas of my life, create my own "genesis," and voluntarily paint my way to a better community, an enriched circle of friends? Am I able to select my paints wisely? Will I choose images of becoming that are appropriate to my potential? Will my canvas be narrow, small and thin, or will I push back the darkness, enlarge the area to be painted, and select more paints and brushes? My canvas will continue to expand, if I am not satisfied. I determine where my canvas ends, because I am the artist of my soul.

That day, with my students, I watched young lives view lives that were. I saw questioning youngsters look for answers in times past. I hope they appreciate that past and the good that came from their ancestors, but I also hope that they never become so secure, safe, and bored with their own lives that they quit searching for improvements in our present world and stop adding to their own individual canvases.

As we left the Joslyn Art Museum, I noticed that each of its bronze doors symbolized one of the six virtues of mankind which forms the periphery of our moral thought as a society: industry, charity, faith, courage, vision, and hope. True art, in whatever form we may like, exemplifies these cornerstones of our development. May it continue to feed our heads, hearts, and souls.

32

Rediscovering Valentine's Day

"The meeting of two personalities
is like the contact of two chemical substances:
if there is any reaction, both are transformed."

-Carl Jung

February 14 is Valentine's Day, the day set aside to celebrate love and the human heart. There are seventeen saints named Valentine listed in the *Roman Catholic Encyclopedia*, and according to Vatican officials, not one is recognized as the patron saint of lovers.

Historians think this yearly celebration springs from ancient Roman festivals celebrating fertility, the Lupercalia Festival and Juno Februata. Others believe it stems from the medieval belief that February 14 marked the beginning of the mating season for birds.

While the origin of the day seems to point to Rome, the day was celebrated chiefly among the English-speaking people. Children of England collected flowers, such as Larkspur, in the summer and pressed them to make wreaths and ornaments for Valentine's Day. Valentines used to consist of plain ribbon bows attached to cards. About one hundred years ago, art stepped in to put more beauty and sentiment into valentines than the homemade articles could produce. Cards began to appear with beautifully embossed borders and messages written inside. It was the proper thing to write a short poem, but unfortunately not everybody could write, so valentine writers appeared.

February, to some, is the last real month of winter. To others, it is Valentine's Day all month long. Besides Black History Month and National Brotherhood Month, February is National Heart Month. For all the attention focused on the heart, the statistics surrounding the heart are truly heartbreaking.

Cardiovascular diseases kill almost as many Americans as all other causes of death combined. Nearly 20% of the American population suffers from this disease. One of every four adults in the United States has high blood pressure. As many as 1.5 million Americans will have a heart attack this year, and one-half million of them will die. These figures point out that people do not know how to take care of their own hearts or how to be nice to the hearts of others. Stephen Crane's poem reminds us of this missing sensitivity:

In the desert
I saw a creature, naked, bestial
Who, squatting upon the ground,
Held his heart in his hands,
And ate of it.

I said, "Is it good, friend?"
"It is bitter, bitter," he answered.
"But I like it
Because it is bitter.
And because it is my heart."

Will we learn to manage our lives so we can take care of ourselves and not eat our own bitter hearts? How many of us get four hugs a day? Tests prove those lucky individuals who receive four or more hugs a day live longer lives. Those who do not get four hugs have a greater chance of eating their own hearts to prevent loneliness.

A student gave me the following letter a few days after I asked his class to turn in a paper about the effects of loneliness. It was written by an old woman, someone's great-grandmother, who he met in a nursing home while visiting someone else:

"God, my hands are old. I never said that out loud before, but they are. I was proud of them once. They were soft like the smoothness of a firm ripe peach. Now, the softness is like worn-out sheets or withered leaves. When did these slender, graceful hands become gnarled and shrunken? When? They lie here in my lap, naked reminders of the rest of this old body that served me well.

How long has it been since someone touched me? Twenty years, I've been a widow, respected, smiled at, but never touched. Never held close to another body. Never held so close and warm that loneliness was blotted out.

I remember how my mother used to hold me, God. When I
was hurt in spirit or flesh, she would gather me close, stroke my silky
hair and caress my back with her warm hands. Oh, God, I'm so lonely!
I remember the first boy who ever kissed me. We were both so new
at that, the taste of young lips and popcorn. The feeling deep inside
of mysteries to come. I remember Hank and the babies. How can I
remember them but together? Out of the fumbling, awkward attempts
of new lovers the babies come, and as they grew, so did our love.

God, Hank didn't seem to care if my body thickened and faded
a little. He still loved it and touched it, and we didn't mind if we were
no longer beautiful, and the children hugged me a lot. God, I'm lonely!

Why didn't we raise the kids to be silly and affectionate, as
well as dignified and proper? They do their duty. They drive up in their
fine cars. They come to my room to pay their respects. They chatter
brightly and reminisce, but they don't touch me. They call me 'Mom' or
'Mother' or 'Grandma.' Never Minnie. My mother called me Minnie,
and my friends. Hank called me Minnie, too, but they're gone, and so is
Minnie. Only Grandma is here. And, God! She's lonely."

Two days after my student got this letter, the lady who wrote
it died. The most insidious disease is loneliness, the ultimate poverty.
Loneliness touches a feeling of no worth and a lack of connectedness.
When people feel they are fighting the world by themselves, they also
feel that they are not loved. We make ourselves lonely by misplacing
our self-worth, building walls around us, and then daring someone to
knock them down, all the while secretly hoping someone does.

The road map of life shows many sharp and unexpected turns,
many hills and steep valleys, a few deserts filled with loneliness, and
wide rivers crossed. When we are alone and troubled, there is a spirit
stronger than us on those narrow roads. Those out-of-the-way places,
which appear to be detours or paths for becoming lost, are the humble
roads that lead us to warm, friendly people where we learn to listen
to the winds of love. All major religions say the same thing. Love
yourself. Love your neighbor as yourself.

On Valentine's Day, touch your friends and family. Hold them.
Feel the beauty of their skin. Listen to their words and their footsteps on
the snow, as they come to you. Touch them with peace and love.

33

Why Laugh Anyway?

"I have faith in the goodness of mankind,
but I'm not overwhelmed by the evidence.
Human beings suffer unjustly; humanity is great . . .
we are saved by understanding and by laughter."

-Primo Levi

I am one of those unfortunate people who have been told he doesn't have a sense of humor. I can easily identify with those who wonder why people are laughing. What is so funny about life anyway? I do try to develop a sense of humor, because so many seem to benefit from having one. I hope to soon find one that fits me, but it has been a long and difficult search.

I am too intense. I am overly concerned about life in general. Tunnel vision afflicts me regularly. Friends tell me to stop and smell the flowers, and I tell them I do not see any, yet I still look for them.

Robert Owen, an American social reformer, said that he found a twelve-year-old boy working in a coal mine and asked him if he knew God. "No," came the reply. "He must work in some other mine." When I hear comments like this, I must make a decision whether to laugh or cry. Sometimes, it is hard to decide which to do.

Much of my childhood was spent on my grandfather's and father's farms north of Rulo, Nebraska. I learned the qualities of surviving in a rural environment. I worked hard. I ate everything I could at each meal, or my stomach hurt a lot before I had a chance to eat again. I drank gallons of water in the summer to deal with the 130-degree heat in the hay barn on humid, August days. I watched carefully where I placed every footfall to avoid snakes in the grass, holes that broke ankles, and manure in the barnyard.

Even then, I noticed that a lot of people were laughing. With so much difficult farm work to do, why would they spend so much time

139

telling funny stories? Why did they act like there was no tomorrow? As I got older, I realized their secret. Tomorrow might not come.

Good people surrounded me, and most of them seemed happy. They were honest and uncomplicated, but most had goals that did not stretch past the horizon.

The one or two dreamers I noticed in this community were the unhappy ones. Their goals reached over the horizon and went out of sight of those who were only concerned about themselves and their own words. The unhappy ones laughed, sometimes, but I could tell their laughter covered up the pain of not fulfilling their dreams. I worried about them and found myself eventually thinking more about the dreamers than the majority who took one day at a time and did not worry themselves about what they could not imagine outside their flat society.

I remember the good times: the ice-cold lemonade on hot days and how cool I felt in the shade of our big oak tree. The home place was on a hill high enough to see the end of Nebraska, and when I climbed to the peak of the barn, that magnificent view introduced me to the beginnings of Kansas, Missouri, and Iowa. I could also watch the barges on the Missouri River, and I dreamed of Huck Finn.

The difference between laughing and crying is a fine line. The memories of my happy childhood become sad ones, when I recall my horse kicking me in the shin and nearly breaking my leg, when I fainted from heatstroke, and when I came close to dying in the barn after a hay stack fell on me. I choose to remember the happy times, but I cannot forget the shadows of some awful moments that still lurk in my memory.

In my youth, I often rode my horse down the county road, beyond the house, across the hilltop, through the timber, down the bluff, and out to the Big Mo. I loved riding and started doing so when I was five years old. Now, when I return and think of that same path, I look differently at the county road. It is such a thin line to be a person's life way: a narrow, dusty, graveled road that barely holds two passing cars.

On the north side of the road are the pastures that my horse ran across and where I skittered through my youth like a colt. For several years, on the south side of that same county road lived Michael Ryan and his friends. This para-military group believed in Yahweh, tortured its enemies, chased neighbors away, partially skinned one of its own members alive, and then caused his death by kicking his chest until his ribs cracked and his heart stopped.

A five-year-old child of another member was chained like an animal to the outside of his trailer house, fed from a dog dish, not allowed to wear any clothes other than underwear, and was swung around by the neck until he choked and his spine broke.

This group not only cracked every bone in the older man's body before burial but forced the child to hold cigarettes in his mouth as they had target practice with their pistols. My father and brother were two neighbors who reported them to the authorities.

On one side of that county road are my memories of happiness. On the other side are ghosts of darkness, perversity, and death. Without our knowing the facts until much later and only three hundred yards from our farm house, this "religious" group buried its victims. More than once, their guards with M-16 rifles stopped my father in his pickup, as he drove down that little county road. They threatened him with death, if he bothered them. Sometimes, it is very hard to have a sense of humor.

One of my fictional idols is Hawkeye Pierce, the character Alan Alda played in the long running television series, *MASH*. I always wanted to be more like Hawkeye, able to find humor in tough situations, conscious of putting people at ease when stress surrounded them, capable of laughing at life's cruelties, and not letting human idiocy affect my principles.

Laughter kept Hawkeye from cracking under the stress of trying to save lives during the Korean War. He was able to help others and make the best of life's sadness in this dangerous time. I wish I could keep my composure, when those around me lose theirs. If only I could find a sense of humor, so I could remember to laugh and not cry, to realize the greatness of humanity, and not succumb to the insanities of our world like the WWII Holocaust and the Ryan's compound.

For the benefit of those who feel that humor and philosophy should not be lumped together, remember what James Thurber said: "If a thing cannot endure laughter, it is not a good thing. Laughter is never out of date or out of place."

Thomas Carlyle also knew its wisdom. "True humor springs not more from the head than the heart; it is not contempt, its essence is love."

The human face requires seventy-two muscles to frown but only fourteen to smile. This means less energy is needed to laugh than cry. Those of us who are short on energy would be wise to see the humor in the world and not focus on its sadness and pain. Laughter may be the only true religious experience that brings us closer to each other and to God.

34

Why Teach English?

"Even if you do learn to speak correct English,
whom are you going to speak it to?"

-Clarence Darrow

"The English language was carefully, carefully cobbled together
by three blind dudes and a German dictionary."

-Dave Kellett

Why would people in their right minds want to teach English in a public high school today? I ask myself this question, frequently. Of all the occupations available to me on this earth, why did I choose to teach this subject and work with teenagers every day? Arriving at this decision was a long process.

I have had many jobs: farm worker, truck driver, gas station attendant, railroad brakeman, sandblaster, an apprentice welder, collection agent, teacher, coach, ice cube cutter, toilet paper salesman, sales manager, and an interim minister. The job of English teacher is the most frustrating and personally satisfying of them all.

In sales, I enjoyed getting a signed contract, and I felt powerful. That feeling was a complicated mask covering the real me. During my last year of that job, six close friends suffered heart attacks and died within a ten-month period. A seventh survived but was forced to alter his lifestyle. I felt like a WWF wrestler on steroids, and I knew I had to change my life.

After eleven years in sales, I returned to what I enjoyed most: reading, writing, and students. I wanted to read as much as I could stand and whenever I chose to do it. I wished to learn as much about the world and myself as I could in the years left to me. I wanted to do something legitimate with the rest of my life.

As my friends began winding up horizontal, my free time was enjoyably spent with my nose stuck in a book, crawling away into a quiet corner, eager to find out what was waiting for me behind the author's words, trying to discover the prize in the next treasure hunt of titles. A kernel of an idea began to form. What would my life be like reading books for a living? Could I do it and survive, financially and emotionally? I began to plan changes in my life.

Three ideas pointed me toward teaching. A thought kept recurring in my waking hours and my nighttime dreams. Jobs should be ones we enjoy, ones we look forward to getting out of bed for in the morning. To work only for the prestige or money involved was slowly becoming a one way ticket to the cemetery. I felt job stress tightening muscles in my chest, altering my attitudes towards those important to me, and changing my personality.

People ought to do what they excel at with no consideration for financial reward. Whether it is running a computer, pumping gas, or sales, if I enjoy it and that is what I do best, then I am cheating myself if I do not do it. Most people can find one area where they achieve. What a waste of our lives not to improve what we do best and see how far we can go towards perfection in that chosen area. As my deceased friends learned, no one knows how long we will live.

As a child, I remember locking myself in my bedroom, so I could read as long as I wanted to and be left undisturbed. My mother still tells stories about me coming into the kitchen after Sunday breakfast and taking the newspaper upstairs, where I could read it alone, quietly. My father, downstairs, bellowed angrily, because he had not finished it before I made my escape.

I made excuses then, and I make excuses in my adult life to find time to read. Where I was from, if a boy did not have a shovel, a hoe, or a ball in his hands, the men in the neighborhood raised their eyebrows. Boys were not caught by their fathers holding an armload of books, when they should be in the hay field, rounding up cattle, or cleaning the horse stalls. I wanted to read wheelbarrows full of books. Teaching and reading are not jobs for me; they are what I would be doing as an avocation, if I worked at something else.

The third reason I chose this occupation is because I have been interested in religions, all of them. There even was a time when

I considered becoming a minister. I do not have what it takes to enter the clergy, because even though religions interest me, churches do not. I feel the values my students learn in the classroom, when reading the best literature, benefits them for life. Too often, priests and ministers wear blinders and adhere to teleological thinking. This causes them to be opposed to new ideas. Literature read with an open mind is non-teleological, eager for new interpretations. This is exciting. It causes the mind to question and the blood to course through the veins more rapidly. Faith often stifles questions, but asking questions is the only way to expand and enlarge one's faith.

Those who study good literature find epiphanies, enlightening experiences similar to worshiping religion. Good literature provides insight into all that is positive and negative in mankind without the necessity of labeling, according to fetishes and symbols. If one reads enough good literature, sooner or later, one feels a presence of a higher spirit, a creative force. Whether the reader opens *Idylls of the King* by Alfred Lord Tennyson, *The Grapes of Wrath* by John Steinbeck, *Leaves of Grass* by Walt Whitman, or *Walden* by Henry David Thoreau, humanity appears to be here for a reason.

Reading good literature is one way of finding out what that reason is. We are finite creatures, but "Art is eternal," as Beethoven said, and for me, the most meaningful art is good literature. In the presence of a good book, I feel humble, warm, emotional, moved, renewed, invigorated, wiser, and uplifted. Religion or the study of it never gave me more than my favorite books of literature have done.

In Chaim Potok's *The Chosen*, the main character, Rueven Malter, and his father discuss the value of an education. The father compliments the son on his grades and ability to learn but warns about keeping all the knowledge to himself.

A few years ago, I read 150 books in twelve months, and I began comparing people and their lives to books. A person's life is like a pen and ink. The body is the pen, and the action of the person is the ink. Some individuals have perfect penmanship when using their ink. Others make an illegible scrawl out of their lives. Some just look at the black lines on the page, trying to fill them up with anything that comes to mind, not worrying about the quality of their products. Some worry about what they write, but others are only anxious about how much white space is left. A few lucky ones discover the meanings between the lines. They peer behind the words to learn what is not seen, to understand what can not be spoken.

I enjoy showing my students they are books themselves. The most important volume in their library is the one they write with their lives. It is not so necessary to fill it with a large number of chapters as it is to make each chapter the best it can be before reaching the last page.

"If the English language made any sense,
a catastrophe would be an apostrophe with fur."

-Doug Larson

35

Writing Well Is Important

"All of us learn to write in the second grade.
Most of us go on to greater things."

-Bobby Knight

It was a new semester. The students filed into class early and were full of anticipation. They smiled a lot, and I smiled back. The students got involved quickly. The lab hummed. There were no show-offs. They all seemed to type well. They knew how to use the computers. The class atmosphere was exceptional. They asked specific questions and understood my comments the first time. I wondered if this might turn out to be an advanced class.

I always look forward to a new class and discovering which students really want to learn, which ones just want a grade, and which ones are looking for a ticket out of town. I share with them my expectations that writing well moves us closer to our potential than most endeavors. Knowledge is power, but good composition leads us to wisdom.

All of a sudden, like thunder in a cloudless sky, there came a question from the back of the room. "Why is writing well so important?"

The question seemed understandable and natural. Anyone could ask it. Any student of any ability might raise this issue. I have heard teachers ask the same thing. This question is the most important one I am asked in English class.

Is writing so important? Do we need good writing? Can it change anything in our lives? The answer is positively, "Yes!" If people can write well, they can change their lives and the world.

Even if students have brilliant ideas or they are great speakers, even if they may be a walking Cicero or a King Solomon, one day in order to introduce their projects or clarify their proposals, they will have to write them down. They will feel helpless, if they are not able to express those great ideas clearly in writing. A wrong word, an immature vocabulary, poor spelling, a breakdown in logic, grammar mistakes - all of these are barriers to career development. No matter what students plan to do with their lives, they should make good composition a part of their daily existence.

Why go this far? Every day we write letters, send email, leave messages, and write advertisements. A nicely composed message full of humor can make a friend forget the offense we caused by chance. A love letter from the bottom of our heart will make even the loneliest person change his/her feelings.

If we want to achieve success, we have to use our writing skills. We must work on them every day using every chance, reading books, writing in a journal, improving mechanics, enriching vocabulary, and learning critical thinking skills, because we will never be able to write well if we cannot think. Never assume that it is too late to begin. Never think that what we write is a waste of time. Try again! One day it will be fine and fun.

The world is a confusing place. What is true? What is false? What seemed right yesterday is wrong today. The art of living well is finding that which is long lasting, even eternal. To live life in search of truth and our own souls is how we ought to measure our lives. Some neighborhoods are littered with physical and emotional trash. However, we can do our part to improve ourselves and clean up our world by not confusing our readers and writing well.

"Thanks for the joy that you've given me. I want you to know that I believe in your song." I remember those lyrics by Dobie Gray. "Help me be strong. Give me the beat, boys, and help me along." Good writing is recording the strong beat of our souls, the music and rhythm that carries us along our paths in life.

"Give me the beat boys and free my soul. I want to get lost in your rock and roll." Oh, to have a passion in life, rock and roll, or any worthwhile occupation, a cause in which to get lost, an opportunity to create, a dream to complete, a chance to heal, a love to be satisfied. Good writing can take us there.

Writing well is poetic. The power of poetry, the impact of a few, well-chosen words can move mountains and deliver an emotional hammer.

The last verse of W. E. Henley's poem, "Invictus," is such an example. "It matters not how straight the gate/How charged with punishment the scroll/I am the master of my fate/I am the captain of my soul."

When a student asks me, "What is the value of writing well?" I think of Aristotle who said the meaning of life is to "know thyself." Writing well is a good way to do that.

No matter the vocation, those who communicate well are most productive. The ability to transfer knowledge and wisdom from one person to another is increased in direct proportion to one's talent in communicating. Writing with a specific motive influences one's opportunity to teach others.

Some have verbal gifts, and talking is their chosen method of communication. Research studies indicate teachers who only lecture reach a significantly small percentage of their students, compared to teachers who use auditory and visual stimulation. If we want what we say to be remembered, we must put our ideas in writing. The better we write, the farther our messages go.

Writing well also comes from reading more. We have proof that good writers are better readers. The opposite is also true. If people want to improve their reading ability, they should write more.

Education is wasted on those who do not know themselves. A simple person who knows what he thinks and why he thinks it is more valuable than an educated fool who has no clue as to his life's mission.

The following shows a world of difference in understanding. The simple addition or removal of a comma can make a sentence mean exactly the opposite of what was intended. A teacher asked his class to make sense out of these words: "a woman without her man is nothing."

A male said the words should read, "A woman, without her man, is nothing."

A female sitting in the next seat said, "A woman! Without her, man is nothing."

Those who write well know the power in a comma and the beauty of a well-written sentence.

"There's no thrill in easy sailing when the skies are clear and blue. There's no joy in merely doing things, which anyone can do. But there is some satisfaction that is mighty sweet to take. When you reach a destination that you thought you'd never make." -Spirella

"Ever tried? Ever failed? No matter. Try again. Fail again. Fail better" (Samuel Beckett).

I am just a man, never perfect. I feel happiest when I am lost in a few chosen words that say clearly what I am thinking. Well-written words provide the opportunity to find a few moments of clarity, a piece of heaven.

E. M. Forster said, "How do I know what I think, until I see what I say?"

Write on.

36

Straight Lines

Questions
A declaration of self
Life in concentrated form
A sentient capacity for feeling
When hearts and spirits touch
A page for the right side of the brain

Infinite
Generally cool
A stress reliever
Happy emotions
God touches another soul
And looks into our eyes

Promise
Opportunity
Good friends
Ordered chaos
Words of wisdom
The fragrant aroma of diamonds

Spirit
Feelings of bliss
Expressions of beauty
Unwrapped between the lines
Healing words dipped in grace
Taking time to admire life's beauty

David Martin

Steam
A necklace of love
Anger and depression
Words beaded together
Imagery communication
Vibrant expectations of the future

Life
World of imagination
Broken-heart medicine
Ballads writing themselves
Blood from wounds unseen
Unheard songs the soul screams

Heart
Not uniform
"What ifs"
Lyrical pictures
A problem solver
Motion in words

Boundless
Portrait of feelings
Capturing moments
A way to write colors
A way to connect with Mom
Emotion forced into straight lines
Hope nestled around dreams of peace

The Wind

flags fluttering freely
grass bending and sycamores sighing
linden laughing and cottonwood crying
hair tossing and weather vanes gyrating
birds' songs carried
to unsuspecting ears

the wind rises and falls
changes direction and intensity
as waves of feeling wash
over me like an upside down ocean

days whistle by with their own momentum, loss and gain
excess and void tickled by the winds of life

blow wind
I don't know where you came from
or where you are going
go wind

pass by and come again
I will be somewhere else then
but you will find me
like a long-lost friend

the cottonwood trees laugh at what they see
noticing the same mistakes made over and over by the same
people wearing different faces

nothing is permanent, except the wind
feel the moment
today will be gone soon
people holding one another
can not last forever
only the wind

David Martin

friends blow away and leave
for worlds unknown
join their revelry
going from here to there
holding all with transparent arms

waves of air caress tree tops
bending blades of grass
felt but not seen
cool to the weary, an act of God
a forerunner of changing seasons
a messenger of early warnings
cloud pusher
shaper of the heavens
listen and learn

whimsical direction
innocent but necessary

Journeys

I fasten my heart to the sun
and let go of past darkness, glowing
inwardly, finding my own warmth
as you travel on a great journey.

My longest sojourns,
all mystical highways,
are not geographic.

Measured in smiles and heartbeats,
not miles and footsteps,
my great journeys
are minute changes in attitude
and redirections of my soul.

David Martin

Sunrise

Before you,
my days were nights.

Now, your smile and touch
push the darkness aside.
With your love,
I feel the dawn unlocking
chains of solitude.

The intensity of your passion
roars up to me,
giving me strength and freedom.

A new day begins.
I feel, at last,
a oneness with the sun and sky.

Too Many

There are too many facts to learn,

too many books to read,

too many jobs to do,

places to go, and

people to please,

so,

today,

the first person

I hugged was me,

and I smiled,

then I laughed

out loud.

David Martin

Woman

Your absence
pulls my skin from its flesh
and reveals empty places
packed with feeling.

Traces of your presence
linger over wine glasses,
opened books, and a rumpled pillow.

The echoes of your voice
make music to my jangled nerves.

The soft breeze I felt
was a ripple of your breath
gently caressing my face.

About *Fine Lines*

Fine Lines, Inc., is a non-profit organization, dedicated to the writing development of authors of all ages. What started out as a classroom newsletter in 1991 has now turned into a 50 state writing network. The first issue was four pages long and allowed students an opportunity to show others their clear thinking and proper written expression. Today, each quarterly issue is filled with fiction, nonfiction, and poetry written by "writers in process" who wish to improve their craft. *Fine Lines* is now in distribution worldwide at WriteLife.com.

Fine Lines receives creative writing from all over the nation and authors of all occupations. Each editon includes prose articles of medium length, reflective essays on widely diverse topics that reflect life experiences, what one learns through the writing process, and poetry in all forms. We have published writers from as far away as Azerbaijan, Canada, China, Denmark, Dubai, England, Germany, Iraq, Japan, Malaysia, Jordan, Sierra Leone, Togo, Turkey, and Switzerland.

To paraphrase George Orwell, good writing is like a window pane, and the editors of *Fine Lines* hope to assist developing writers see through their windows more clearly. Our mission is to help writers develop their full potential.

We invite readers to develop their full potential and submit writing to *Fine Lines*. Our submission guidelines can be found at www.finelines.org. Remember Horace's words, "He who has hit upon a subject suited to his powers will never fail to find eloquent words and lucid arrangement."

Write on,

David Martin
President
Fine Lines, Inc.

fine-lines@cox.net

www.finelines.org